WiccaCraft for Families

WiccaCraft for Families
The Path of the Hearthfire

by
Margie McArthur

PHOENIX PUBLISHING INC.

This edition printed 1994

PHOENIX PUBLISHING, INC.
Portal Way
P.O. Box 10
Custer, Washington USA 98240

Distributed in Canada by
PHOENIX PUBLISHING INC.
#276; 20465 Douglas Crescent
Langley, B.C. V3A 4B6

ISBN 0-919345-52-2

Cover design by Rick Testa
Illustrations by Lorna Lake

Printed in the U.S.A.

This book has been manufactured on recycled paper using vegetable based inks.

Contents

Introduction   9

Part 1 - The Basics

CHAPTER 1   The Sabbats   15
CHAPTER 2   Altars and Rituals   21
CHAPTER 3   The Natural World   27

Part 2 - Ways of Celebration

CHAPTER 4   The Magic of Home   37
CHAPTER 5   Samhain   45
CHAPTER 6   Yule   63
CHAPTER 7   Imbolc   85
CHAPTER 8   Ostara   99
CHAPTER 9   Beltane   113
CHAPTER 10   Litha   133
CHAPTER 11   Lughnasadh   147
CHAPTER 12   Mabon   161
CHAPTER 13   Moontides and Magic   173
CHAPTER 14   Prayers   181

Part 3 - Rites of Passage

CHAPTER 15   Women's Mysteries   189
CHAPTER 16   Men's Mysteries   197
CHAPTER 17   Youth Passages   209
CHAPTER 18   Handfasting   227
CHAPTER 19   Age   239
CHAPTER 20   Death   245

               Bibliography   254
               Suggested Reading   255
               Resources   263
               About the Author   267

ACKNOWLEDGMENTS

Many wonderful friends have contributed in ways large and small to the writing of this book. It is impossible to name them all; my love and thanks go out to them nonetheless. I would like to especially thank the following major contributors:

JoAnn Adams — for years of friendship, sisterhood, support, and for her expertise and help in creating many happy communal Sabbats for our children. Special thanks for allowing me to use some of the ceremonies she wrote for these occasions.

Ed Fitch — for friendship, scholarly research, and allowing me free use of his works, published and unpublished. The pagan community may never know just how much this beloved "Grandfather of the Craft" has contributed to the neo-pagan renaissance.

Janina Renee — for friendship and sisterhood through our years of childraising, for folklore expertise and scholarship second to none.

Phillip Wayne — for his generosity, encouragement, hours of hard work, and musical genius.

Morgyn Owens-Celli — for his kindness in supplying the wheat-weaving information.

Joy Gardner Gordon and Crossing Press — for kindly allowing me to share her Crystal Energization Technique.

Marian Geraghty — for years of friendship and for use of her music, as well as the Blessing and Night Prayer.

Dancers of the Mist Coven — for kindly sharing their Beltane Ritual with me.

Sven Coman-Luger — for allowing me to use his Rite of Handfasting.

Wren and Gryphon — dear friends, for allowing me to use their Summer Solstice Handfasting Rite.

Nemeton and The Church of All Worlds — for allowing me to use "Lughnasadh Dance" and "Harvest Dance" by Gwydion.

Kayendres — for sharing the Mohawk Feast of the Dead and other teachings.

Michael Tierra — for his gracious contribution to the chapter on herbs.

Brooke Medicine Eagle — for permission to quote from her article "Grandmother Lodge."

Caer Cailleach — our "home" coven and cauldron of many an inspiration.

Plough Publishing — for permission to use "Harvest Song," music by Marlys Swinger, copyright 1972.

Abingdon Press — for permission to use "Jack-O'Lantern" from *Songs for the Little Child*, copyright 1921; copyright renewal 1949 by Clara Belle Baker.

J. Paul Espinoza of Golden Bough — for permission to use his arrangement of "The Woodcutter's Song."

To Brigid: Hearth Fire Goddess of my Irish ancestors.

To the beautiful green Earth and all the beings thereon and therein: the two-leggeds, the four-leggeds, the eight-leggeds; the winged ones, the finned ones, the crawling ones, the flowering ones; the Standing People, the Stone People, the Devas, the Nature Spirits, the Fairy People. May we live in the knowledge that we are all related! May we ever live in harmony! Blessed Be!

To my family: Bran, Althea, Dylan, Sunflower and Emrys, without whom this book would not be. Blessed Be!

INTRODUCTION

I must admit that I'm not much of a child of the modern age. Plastics, television and the rapid pace of modern life are not my cup of tea. But then again, I've grown fond of my word processor, and if I didn't have it and a dishwasher I wouldn't be sitting here writing this book.

But to get back to my original feelings and how they concern the subject of this book....

Those of us calling ourselves "Pagan" or "Wiccan" in these final years of the twentieth century have a unique responsibility if we have chosen to have children. Our responsibility is to raise our children in a way that will heal the past and create a viable future. The desecration and desacralization of the earth is a fact of our lives. The earth has been (and continues to be) grievously wounded by our thoughtless lack of awareness of our true relationship with Her and with all life. These subjects have been dealt with at length in many fine books and it is beyond the scope of this one to deal with them here. There are, however, some statements that I feel I need to make.

What is it to be pagan, to be Wiccan? It is to embrace a cosmic world view that holds that the Earth is a living, sentient being, following Her own course of evolution, both physically, and in one's consciousness. To be pagan is to realize that we, along with all other life forms on the planet, are an integral part of Her and of this plan. It is to realize that everything, from the smallest gnat to the largest galaxy is linked, connected in the web of life, and that because of this connectedness, our actions on one level can and do have effects on other levels. We therefore must act in a responsible manner.

To be pagan is a lifestyle, a way of being that encompasses one's whole life on a daily basis. Being pagan is not just a set of mental constructs, wherein God the Stern Father becomes Goddess the Loving Mother and we all get to throw off the oppressive patriarchy and complain self-righteously about our Judeo-Christian upbringing and culture.

To be pagan is to recognize deeply the feminine and masculine principles of the Divine as they manifest throughout the many realities. It is to see beyond them both to the Oneness of the life force. It is to see and rejoice in the sheer magnitude, beauty, and diversity of individualities manifested by this life force. It is to live daily inside the realization of the interrelatedness of all life and to "walk your talk" in this regard.

Walking your talk is a very individual thing, but for all of us it means being more conscious, not just (and not always) politically correct in the many choices we are called on daily to make. For pagans it has to mean embracing a more natural and wholistic lifestyle, otherwise we are just "talking", not "walking."

The pace of twentieth century life makes it very hard to have a relationship with the nonhuman beings who inhabit this planet. We've allowed plastic and vinyl to replace the natural substances that used to surround us. As a culture we have lost our sense of connectedness to the earth and all her creatures, our place in the natural scheme of things.

To regain a more natural lifestyle takes real work and dedication. Our family has been working on it for years, and I know there is still more room for improvement. We have switched from plastic toys to toys made from natural materials that have warmth, life, and integrity to them, as well as the beautiful, natural colors of the rainbow, the flowers, and the earth, sea and sky. Cotton, wool and other natural fibers are replacing synthetics in our clothing, bedding, even our curtains. It is neither possible, nor desirable, to replace every artificial fiber in our lives, but we should aim to make conscious and well-reasoned choices about the products we use, and to what degree they are in agreement with the ecological ideals of our pagan philosophy of life. Television viewing has been largely replaced with pastimes like reading aloud, drawing pictures, singing, playing games and other creative activities; the kids don't even miss it anymore.

Our ways of caring for ourselves have also changed over the years. We now assume more responsibility for our health, instead of immediately turning it over to a doctor. We've learned the way of herbs, of vibrational medicines, of energy movement techniques such as acupuncture and the Touch for Health system, and the value of an occasional fast. Doctors are a wonderful resource when we need them, but most often we don't. It is very empowering to get to know your own body (as well as the bodies of your children) well enough to be able to read its language and interpret its needs.

Last, but not least, to my way of thinking, a pagan lifestyle that does not include natural foods is a contradiction in terms. Conscious choice in regard to the nourishment and care of our bodies is Grounded Spirituality on an everyday basis. A natural foods diet is one based upon simple, wholesome and relatively unprocessed, seasonally available foods—whole grains, vegetables, fruits, nuts, beans and, if desired, occasionally meat (a vegetarian diet just doesn't work for everybody). Pagans eating a regular diet of junk food strikes me about the same way as styrofoam at a Sabbat picnic. If we are not consciously loving and caring of our physical beings in this way, is it then surprising that we are equally unconscious in our care of the body of our Earth Mother?

I realize that our family's way of doing things is not for everyone; we are each different, with different needs. But as pagan parents, if we don't teach our children about the natural world and their relationship to it, we are not fulfilling our duties. We need to achieve a balance, neglecting neither our duty to see that they grow up as well balanced, responsible citizens of our society, nor their responsibilities to Mother Earth to see that She lives and thrives.

It is my hope that this book will help you impart to your children a reverence for nature, an appreciation of our history and folkways, a love of ritual and celebration, and a sense of awe, wonder and joy for this great gift of life.

PART 1

The Basics

CHAPTER 1

THE SABBATS

There are many different mythologies associated with the diverse traditions of paganism. But one thing that all traditions have in common is a celebration of the Sabbats. The Sabbats are the eight ancient festivals—the solstices, the equinoxes, and the cross-quarter days—that mark the turning of the wheel of the year. They indicate important points in the solar cycle, the changing of the seasons and the cycle of plant and animal life in the natural world.

Essentially, the basic themes of the Sabbats are birth, life, death, repose and rebirth. No matter what mythological tradition is applied, these are the recurring points.

The God has two aspects: the god of the waxing year, whose time of influence is from the Winter Solstice until the Summer Solstice, and is referred to as the Oak King; and the god of the waning year, whose time of influence is from the Summer Solstice until the Winter Solstice when he is referred to as the Holly King. The God is symbolic of the sun and his life cycle is a reflection of the vegetation cycle of the earth. He is also Lord and Protector of the Animals. His energy has much "animal" in it, and he is frequently depicted wearing horns, and surrounded by creatures of the wild. He is sometimes depicted as the Ruler of the Underworld, the Land of Death, and death in life (sleep, trance, etc.).

The Goddess is eternal in the sense that she never experiences death. But she also changes her aspect during the course of the year. The Maiden of spring becomes the fertile Earth Mother who brings the bounty of the harvest, who becomes the Crone of late fall and winter. At the Winter Solstice the aspects overlap as she becomes the mother of the infant sun. For a very thorough treatment of this please read the introduction to *Eight*

Sabbats For Witches by Janet and Stewart Farrar (published by Phoenix Publishing, Inc.). Actually, read the entire book—it is excellent.

Sabbats are times of celebration, times of feasting, times of keeping in touch with what is happening in nature. The aspect of being in touch with the natural cycle makes them fire festivals. Every Sabbat is a fire festival, as fire is a symbol of the sun. Ancient pagan sabbats were celebrated with bonfires, and when this was not possible, with the use of torches. Light and heat are elements essential to human survival. The sacred marriage of sun and earth is the cause of life on earth. So this is what each Sabbat celebration is about: Life on earth, as manifested in the amount of light and heat, as well as the fertility of earth and all her creatures. In these days of human overpopulation the fertility referred to is not just physical; it also means the fertility of ideas, creativity in many realms of life. The rituals in this book are enhanced by use of a bonfire during the summer months, a large candle in a cauldron during the winter months (the bonfire brought indoors), plenty of candles, and (if you have a fireplace) a hearthfire.

Some of the rituals are meant to be celebrated around another item central to our lives: the family table. In celebrating the result of earth's fertility we celebrate the abundance she gives us. So we feast, we make merry, all the while remembering our Mother, our Father, and thanking them. The table, decorated with the bounty of nature, interspersed with candles, keeps us ever mindful of the reason for our merriment.

The Sabbats occurring on the Wheel of the Year can be divided roughly into three categories. Imbolc, Ostara and Beltane are Spring-Summer feasts; they are related to the planting and flowering season. Lughnasadh, Mabon and Samhain are Fall-Winter feasts; they are related to the harvest and death season. (Actually, Imbolc falls in the winter and Lughnasadh falls in the summer but in both festivals the theme is one of foreshadowing the approaching season, hence my categorization.) The solstices of Yule and Litha are the axis upon which the Wheel turns; they celebrate the birth and death of the sun in its dual-god aspects of the waxing and waning year.

If everything is frozen solid at Ostara in your location, perhaps you should use Beltane to celebrate spring. On the other hand, if everything is in bloom by Imbolc, definitely it is time for you to celebrate the arrival of spring at this time of the year.

The rituals in this book are by way of suggestion. Feel free to adapt them to your own needs, to your own climate. You may not need all of them. You may want to combine elements of two or three of them into one ritual to better reflect the reality of where you live. Make them your own, create a cycle for your family, but most of all, have fun with them.

For the purposes of this book the following mythological cycle is suggested:

At YULE (December 21st), the darkest time of the year, we mark the passing (death) of the god of the waning year, and the birth of his twin/other self, the god of the waxing year. He is referred to as the Child of Promise. The promise is that of the return of long hours of sunlight and the bounty of the earth.

At IMBOLC (February 2nd) we truly notice the lengthening of the days, and also the first stirring of (vegetative) life within the belly of the Earth Mother. We honor the light and the promise of life.

At OSTARA (March 21st) the light has gained ground and is now equal with the dark. The first signs of plant growth are now seen in the natural world (depending on where you live, of course). We mark Ostara by celebrating the birth of the God in his vegetation and animal aspect, as well as rejoicing in the return of the Maiden and the lengthening of days.

At BELTANE (May 1st) the Sun God matures into a young man and becomes the lover of the Goddess. He impregnates her with the child who will be born at the Winter Solstice (himself). At Beltane we celebrate fertility and sexuality, as well as the fact that the daylight hours now outnumber the hours of darkness. Beltane was the beginning of summer for the Celts, directly opposite Samhain on the Wheel of the Year. It, like Samhain, was a time when the veil between the worlds was thin, and coming and going between them was easier than during the rest of the year. It was not unlikely that fairies or other spirits would be seen during this time.

At LITHA (June 21st), when the light of the Sun God is at its peak, he is challenged and defeated by his twin/other self, the god of the waning year. From now on the hours of daylight will become shorter. The crops already planted will continue to grow, will be harvested, and will be put into the granaries of the tribe. But things have changed with the ascendancy of the Holly King, the god of the waning year, and even in the midst of the abundance, we will notice it.

At LUGHNASADH (August 1st) we observe how the days have short- ened, we have a wake for the dead god, we celebrate the first fruits of the harvest and we mark the time of the mating of the Goddess with the God of the waning year. The child she bears will be born at the following Ostara and is representative (at Ostara) of the lengthening hours of daylight and the sowing and/or first growth of the seeds that will become the fall harvest.

At MABON (September 22nd), as the days grow even shorter and dark hours begin to outnumber those of light, we are aware that the dead god is descending to the underworld. We celebrate the abundance nature offers us, we rest from our labors (those of the planting and harvesting seasons). We look around and see the vegetation beginning to die off. We see the wild animals beginning to store foods for winter and we know the cold, dark times are not far off.

At SAMHAIN (October 31st) the days are very short. The cold weather is upon us. The gate of the underworld swings open to receive the soul of the dead god and the souls of all the animals who are culled from the herds at this time of year. Because the gate to the underworld is open, the other spirits residing there may also come and go. We honor our departed friends and relatives, as well as the Mighty Dead at this time of year. The god rests in the underworld, awaiting rebirth at Yule.

At YULE (December 21st) the god of the waning year, the Holly King, now seen as an old man, dies and his twin/other self, the Oak King, god of the waxing year is reborn, thus bringing us full circle again.

Since one picture is frequently worth more than a thousand words please see the accompanying diagram to better explain these last thousand words.

In this book, since the aim is to work with children, I have tried to keep the themes simple. Simplicity and symbolism is the language that is best understood by children. They will learn more through these methods than through a complex, scholarly explanation of the themes of the Sabbats. The older the child the more intellectual the approach can be. Some of the rituals are more complex than others because I realize this book will be used by people whose children are of varying ages. Feel free to make whatever changes in the material you desire, so that it will meet your family's needs.

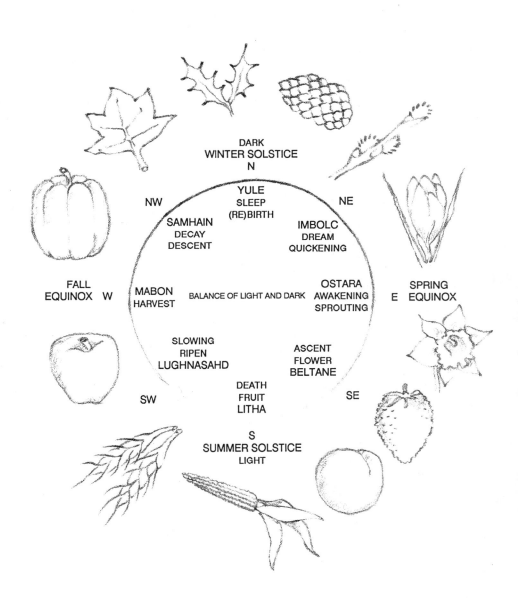

DARK
WINTER SOLSTICE
N

NW

NE

YULE
SLEEP
(RE)BIRTH

SAMHAIN
DECAY
DESCENT

IMBOLC
DREAM
QUICKENING

FALL
EQUINOX   W

MABON
HARVEST

BALANCE OF LIGHT AND DARK

OSTARA
AWAKENING
SPROUTING

E   SPRING
EQUINOX

SLOWING
RIPEN
LUGHNASAHD

ASCENT
FLOWER
BELTANE

SW

DEATH
FRUIT
LITHA

SE

S
SUMMER SOLSTICE
LIGHT

CHAPTER 2
ALTARS AND RITUALS

Doing a ritual involves creating a sacred space. Since all spaces are of the God/dess they are inherently sacred already, so what does it mean to create sacred space? What it means is to bring ourselves into alignment with the continuously existing sacredness that is already present. We bring our consciousness to bear on this and arrange our physical environment in such a way as to create first a stillness within, and next, the alignment we desire. In other words, we set up an altar, create an "environment" (sweeping, smudging, etc.), ground and center ourselves, acknowledge the powers of creation and cast our circle. Thus the inner and outer worlds become reflections of one another, overlap, and we are in the space "between the worlds."

Doing this with children is both simple and challenging. It is simple because children are more naturally attuned to a larger reality than adults; challenging, because it forces us to give up many of our concepts of the "way things are supposed to be done."

In working with my children over the last several years I have found that the physical elements of this are extremely important. Children are newly incarnate—they are trying to get used to, and become comfortable (again!) in the physical world. Talking at them about these matters meets with limited success unless I am talking in a way that sets fire to their imaginations and/or engages their bodies. More successful is a method that combines the power of the eloquently spoken word with the beauty of a candlelit room and the drifting smoke of the incense, the physical act of walking the circle with the rhythmic intonation of a story well told or a song well sung.

Here is a grounding/centering exercise we use at home and when we work with other groups. It involves a short visualization wherein we picture ourselves growing roots (from the soles of our feet and from our root chakra area) as if we were trees. We allow our roots to grow deep into the earth, feeling them move through the soil, down through the layers to the fiery core—the fireheart—of the earth; then we anchor them there. We allow earth energy to move upward through these roots and into our bodies, suffusing us with the vital, nourishing energy of the earth. We feel this energy mix with our own energy and move up our spinal cords and out of the top of our heads where it connects with an energy corridor that spirals from our crown chakra area through the sky, upward, through the sun, past the stars, along the spiralling arm of the Milky Way galaxy to its very center—the central sun. We feel the energy from this as it flows down the spiralling corridor and into our bodies—mixing with the earth energy (as well as our own) and down our roots into the earth. We feel how the energies flow both ways. We feel ourselves filled with these energies, and feel ourselves related to both earth and sky, dark and light, Goddess and God. We join hands and energies with those next to us and feel our connectedness, thus moving the energy from the purely vertical to include the horizontal. Then we stretch out our hands and let this energy pour into the ground—as a give-back, a way of returning some of what we have received.

We place a good deal of emphasis on the physical environment we create for our ceremonies, making it as beautiful and special as possible that we might engage the children's imagination and interest. Altars in particular are a big focus for us since the altar (always the symbolic center of our circle) is the visual focal point of the ceremony.

There are a variety of altar options available for those of you using this book. For as many of the rituals as possible, the family dining table is the altar of choice because the ritual involves a feast. Some of the rituals are designed to be done by the hearthfire, so the area in front of the hearth could be used as an altar, or a cloth on the floor close by the hearth. If you have no fireplace you will definitely need the cloth-on-the-floor altar, or a coffee table, with a large candle symbolic of the hearthfire. Some of the rituals are to be done outside, and again, a cloth on the ground, of a seasonal color, can become an altar. When the dining table is our altar we always use a special, seasonally colored or decorated tablecloth as an altar cloth. Through the years I've made them one by one, and now we have quite a nice collection.

As far as altar equipment goes, the elaborate layout used for adult-type rituals is totally unnecessary. We have found that for family rituals simplicity is best. Needed are God and Goddess symbols (which can be statues, pine cones, sheaves of grain, acorns, seashells, rocks, etc.), water and salt (these represent the elements of water and earth and are used to bless and consecrate the participants), incense (a smudge stick or branch of sage will do; symbolic of both the fire and air elements, also used for consecrating people), candles (for light, beauty, the element of fire, and seasonal symbolism), flowers and herbs of the season, a libation bowl (for food and drink offerings to the deities) and of course whatever seasonal decorations and power objects you wish to have around.

Children love pageantry and ritual and I have designed the rituals to include active participation by children. In some cases your older children can do the entire ritual (most of the plays fall into this category). Younger children can be given jobs like lighting candles (with assistance, of course), putting out candles (a candle snuffer is a fun thing to have), carrying around the salt and water or the incense to help bless people, ringing bells or rapping on the ground with a staff when it is called for in the ritual, and holding props or the scripts for the older children.

Costumes for the plays are a must. They needn't be complex and difficult. The children can even help in the construction of masks, crowns, capes, etc. It helps to purchase a basic robe pattern at your local fabric store. These are always available around Halloween time. They can be made up in different colors and serve as costumes or robes for priests, priestesses, wizards, queens, and anyone else who wears a robe. Sometimes the patterns will also come with crown, wings, wands or wizard hat patterns in the same envelope. A length of colored or white drapery cord can serve as a sash or belt. Swords and shields can be put together by anyone with a minimum of wood-working experience, or plastic ones (only if necessary!) can be purchased in most toy stores. Masks can be made out of paper bags or cardboard from old boxes, painted the color you want, and fastened onto the child by means of an elastic band stapled to either side of the mask. Or take a trip to your local second-hand store and poke around for costume-type clothing and old jewelry. Children so much love dressing up that it is very worthwhile to provide costumes for their plays and rituals. It makes the whole thing more exciting, meaningful and memorable for them.

In our house we have an old toybox that has come to be known as the costume box. It is filled with old tunics, robes, fancy dresses, capes, sashes, veils, crowns, and Halloween costumes. It is somewhat like a treasure chest full of surprises. I never know quite what the kids are going to put together from its contents, but I am usually pleasantly surprised. It is a wonderful resource to have around for everyday playing, but it really proves its worth when, with only a bit of scavenging around in it, we turn up just the perfect thing for a wizard or a dragon to wear.

If you choose not to use a dining table for an altar, preferring to work in a circle, please decorate the circle boundaries with seasonal items. It will beautify the area and add to the atmosphere of specialness. The following list of suggestions may be helpful:

SAMHAIN: dry, colored leaves, nuts, sprigs of dried herbs, small pumpkins, pomegranates, acorns to outline the circle, with large jack-o'lanterns or perhaps dried corn stalks at the four quarters. Photos or mementos of deceased friends and relatives could also be placed at the quarters along with an orange candle to represent the undying spirit.

YULE: pine cones, evergreen boughs, sprigs of holly, ivy, oak, and or mistletoe (since mistletoe is poisonous it is not advisable to use at ground level if you have small children or curious pets), holly-decorated red candles or wreaths laid on the ground with candles inside at the four quarters.

IMBOLC: any early white flowers (allysium, narcissus, etc.) or votive candles to outline the circle, with large white candles, surrounded by a sampling of any green buds and shoots available, and some seeds at the four quarters.

OSTARA: budding branches (pussy willow would be beautiful), early greenery and flowers, with baskets of colored eggs and pale green candles at the four quarters.

BELTANE: flowers, blossoms and greenery to outline the circle, with beribbonned baskets of flowers and large candles of a pastel flower shade at the four quarters.

LITHA: candle lanterns, oak leaves and small branches, yellow and orange flowers, with flower encircled golden, red, orange, or yellow candles at the four quarters, or beribbonned bunches of yellow yarrow or marigolds at the four quarters, beside the candle.

LUGHNASADH: stalks or sheaves of wheat, barley or other grains, sprigs of sweet smelling and or flowering herbs, "sun-colored" flowers, baskets of flowers and whatever fruit is ripe in your area, accompanied by red or orange candles at the four quarters. Also, small round "sun-faced" loaves of bread could be put at the quarters.

MABON: gourds, Indian corn, apples, nuts, squashes, colored leaves (if available this early in your area), vines and ivy tendrils, with piles or baskets of fruit (blackberries are traditional this time of year) around the red-orange quarter candles.

For Moon celebrations the following decorative ideas are suggested:

FULL MOON:

On occasions when it is not possible to be outdoors to celebrate this event, position a mirror within the circle in such a manner as to reflect the full moon from a nearby window.

Use a silver or white altar cloth, or perhaps one that is the color of the night sky with a white, round moon sewn on. Use white candles. Notice what sign of the zodiac the moon is in and include the symbolism of that sign somewhere in your decor. For example, if the moon is in the earthy, Venus-ruled sign of Taurus, you would want to have colorful flowers, leafy branches, and other beautiful, earthy types of objects on the altar or outlining the circle.

For ritual cakes bake (or buy) white (or pale colored), round cookies. I have included a recipe for our Full Moon Almond Cookies in the Moontides and Magic chapter.

Use silver or silver colored implements for the altar: cups, plates, etc.

DARK MOON:

A dark blue or black altar cloth, perhaps embroidered with stars, and dark candles. Again, notice what sign the moon is in and represent it in your circle.

For ritual cakes add carob or chocolate powder to the above mentioned Almond Cookies and they become Dark of the Moon Cookies.

NEW MOON:

A dark altar cloth, as above, but with a crescent moon sewn or embroidered on to it. Dark or silvery candles can be used. The Carob Almond Cookie recipe can be used and shaped into crescents.

CHAPTER 3

THE NATURAL WORLD

PETS

Children should be encouraged and allowed to have pets if it all possible. The experiences of knowing, loving and relating to an animal and the responsibility of caring for its physical needs are essential ones if children are to grow to the understanding that all creatures on the earth are brothers and sisters, children of the Great Mother.

Frequently children feel a pull toward a particular kind of animal as a pet—cat, dog, rabbit, wolf, bear, dragon. Attention should be paid to these preferences. It may not be possible to have certain animals as pets (a dragon, bear or wolf in the back yard could be the cause of annoyed neighbors at the very least, if not a visit from city authorities!), but try to see that the child learns as much as he or she desires about these animals, not just their physical routines and life-styles, but the essence, the inner natures of them. These qualities can be learned better through stories, fables and symbolism than through scientific text. Often when a child relates strongly to a particular animal that animal is a power animal or guardian for the child. A child can have more than one power animal, and can also "grow out" of one animal and into another.

Children should be encouraged to communicate with their pets and with animals in general. Children are naturally psychic and can be easily taught (if they do not already know) to send waves of love and good feelings to animals. A little harder to teach, but still possible, is to receive communication from the animals (some children know and do this instinctively). Tell them to just listen with their inner ear, or to sense what the animal is saying. Tell them the messages often come in the form of feelings.

Try to form the habit with your children of having a nightly quiet time when you sit with the animals, stroking them and, with your imaginations, projecting your consciousness into their minds, trying to fathom their thoughts and feelings. Similarly, let the animals into your mind and consciousness.

Most of all, tell your children often (by your deeds as well as your words) to appreciate and love their animal friends, and to show that appreciation with gifts of caring, love and appropriate food.

Children who have allergies and cannot have animals in the home can still have magical pets. Do you remember the story of the Velveteen Rabbit? A stuffed animal can be a real and dear friend for a child. Or perhaps you might want to quilt, embroider, knit, crochet, draw or sculpt an animal. Embellish it often. Talk to it. Treat it as if it were a real, living animal and it will live and be as beneficial for that child as a real animal would be.

PLANTS, GARDENS AND RECYCLING

Much that was said in the previous section about animals could be restated here concerning plants.

Children can and should be encouraged to grow plants, and develop some type of relationship with them. Whether you have enough land for a full scale garden or only room for a flowerpot, it is important for children to experience the miracle of life in this way. To plant something, take care of it, watch it grow, learn its needs, talk to it, harvest and make use of it with respect, teaches much about life on this planet, and particularly our pagan way of life and values.

Children can see devas, fairies and nature spirits much easier than most adults. Encourage them to dance with, sing to, and draw "the little people in the flower garden," especially under the full moon in May when the little people are quite active.

Encourage them to communicate with the little people, to leave out gifts of food or something that is a token of themselves. Read to them, from the old fairy tales, of encounters between humans and other kingdoms of nature. (If you wish to pass on a true and ancient pagan heritage to your children, read to them often from the old fairy tales and folk tales. I realize that a lot of them are replete with stereotypically wicked witches and child-eating giants; none the less, many old pagan beliefs and customs, as well as fragments of initiatory traditions of the Goddess are preserved in these little gems.)

Encourage them to use their imaginations to take journeys into the fairy kingdom, into flowers, trees, plants and respectfully visit with the people they meet there. Most especially, help them to realize that these little people are their relatives, since we are all children of one Mother.

Take walks in a natural setting as frequently as possible, being aware of the season of year and time of day and how this relates to what is there. Use your senses to the fullest to tune into the plants—color, scent, texture, and, if safe, taste.

Building a compost heap is a sacred act, as is recycling. Being involved with plants helps children to learn the interconnectedness of all life forms. If you have room on your property for even a small compost heap and a few boxes for recycling bottles, cans and jars, I highly recommend it.

It is possible to communicate with plants. Just sit by them in a quiet, open, loving and meditative state and see what comes through to you. Sometimes they speak quite loudly, such as when you forget to water them. The plants will speak to you of their essential energies, and sometimes will make suggestions as to how they can assist you in your life. For an interesting and thorough treatment of the subject of communication with plant devas please read *Behaving As If the God in All Life Mattered* and *The Perelandra Garden Book* by Machaelle Small Wright (see Suggested Readings)

Please try to find room in your life for plants!

COLORS AND CRYSTALS

With all the crystal consciousness abounding these days, I'm sure very few people reading this book do not number among their belongings a quartz crystal or two.

Rocks and crystals make wonderful gifts for children. Who could resist the sparkling beauty or wonderful colors of the various crystals available just about everywhere today? The Native Americans believe that rocks are conscious beings, although with a consciousness different than ours. Rocks are denser beings than we are and their vibratory rate is quite different. As with plants and animals, a relationship should be formed with them, but it will be a different one. And, as with all relationships, love and respect are important elements. This appreciation for the crystal beings, their friendship, and the powerful gifts they bring to us, is an essential and integral part of the relationship. Crystals should not be used in an unconscious or careless manner, nor should they be collected as mere specimens to adorn one's shelves.

When a crystal comes into your life, the first thing to do with it is to give thanks. If you have mined the crystal yourself, leave a small offering of thanksgiving in the place from which the crystal was taken. If, like most of us these days, you purchase your crystal, let the thanksgiving offering to the earth be conducted in your own yard or a favorite outdoor spot. The offering can be in the form of tobacco or cornmeal. Lacking these, a simple and heartfelt offering of your own love and energy directed to the earth would be suitable.

See what impressions you receive from the crystal. What does it tell you about itself, its function? The crystal should then be "cleansed," that is, cleared of any negative vibrations it might have collected and stored prior to coming to you. Crystals can be cleansed by burying them in the earth for three to four days, soaking them (outdoors) in a solution of sea salt and water for three to four days, smudging them with sage smoke, or by intention—holding them in your hands with an intention of clarity, then blowing forcefully on them.

There are many good books currently in print about the occult and healing powers of crystals and other stones. I've listed some for you in the Suggested Reading section.

Wearing and using stones and crystals is something I do, and something I encourage my children to do. I feel stones are a wonderful adjunct to our healing tools, and will come to be even more appreciated in the future.

I begin sharing the world of healing with color and crystals with my children by explaining to them about the chakric system. I keep it simple, showing them the physical locations of each chakra, and pointing out which organs of the body would be affected by an imbalance of energy in a particular chakra. Then we talk about the colors associated with each chakra, and how that color feeds and nourishes that part of the body. I tell them to visualize those certain colors surrounding and penetrating that part of their bodies when they feel the need. I show them my various stones and demonstrate how they can lay these stones on themselves or whoever they are working with, and tell them how both the color and the power of the stone will speed up the healing process. Then I add the final step of showing them how to use their hands and their breath to channel energy into the person, letting it go wherever the body decides to use it.

Kids are great at this! They haven't had years of being brainwashed that this kind of stuff is hokum, so they just go ahead and DO it. Working with crystals, stones and colors is a wonderful way to keep them in touch with their own psychic sensitivity and intuition, as well as training them (subtly) in visualization and equipping them with tools which can be used to help themselves and others.

Crystals can be used for energy enhancement while bathing or while resting. In her book *Color and Crystals*, Joy Gardner tells of a simple energization technique that involves laying down and resting within a simple gridwork of quartz crystals. Pick a time when you can be relatively undisturbed for twenty minutes. Take the phone off the hook. Use four single terminated crystals and make sure the points are towards you. Lay them out, two to six inches away from your body. Put one to the right of your right wrist, one at the left of your left wrist, one between and below your feet and one above the center of the top of your head. Then lay down with your head in the north and rest for twenty to forty minutes.

For much valuable information on the use of crystals read Joy's book (above) as well as the other listed in the Suggested Reading section.

HERBS

I will say only a few words about herbalism; it is too vast a subject to deal with in any depth here. There are many wonderful books on the subject (see Suggested Reading section). My personal favorites are *The Holistic Herbal* by David Hoffman, *The Family Herbal* by Barbara and Peter Theiss, *The Way of Herbs* and *Planetary Herbology* by Michael Tierra, and *The Herbs of Life* by Lesley Tierra for medicinal herbs, and any of Scott Cunningham's books on magical herbalism. Rosemary Gladstar, founder of the California School of Herbal Studies, has written a beautiful, information-packed Herbal Correspondence Course. Michael and Lesley Tierra, herbalists, acupuncturists, teachers, and authors, have written a wonderfully comprehensive correspondence course on Planetary Herbalism. For further information on both of these courses, write to the authors. Their addresses will be found in the Resources section in the back of this book.

Exposing children to the wonderful world of herbs is a continuation of their education about plants. Include an herb garden with the rest of your plants. Involve your children in planting and harvesting rituals, done according the lunar cycle.

Fresh herbs can be used in cooking. They also can be soaked in olive oil to make medicinal oils; gently heating them and blending in some beeswax turns the oil into a healing salve. Toss a few sprigs into a cup of boiling water, steep five minutes and you have tea. Put herbs in a large jar of water and set it out in the sun and make sun tea. Or set it out by the light of the full moon and make moon tea. The two, though they may contain the same herbs, will be subtly different. When you learn the lore of herbs, it is possible to make wonderfully healing brews.

Dry herbs by hanging them up, flowering ends down, in medium-sized bunches tied together with string. Hang them in a dark, dry area that gets a lot of air circulation. When they are dried they can be used to flavor foods, to make incenses, to make bathbags, potpourris, sachets, etc.

Every Yule my children and I make herbal gifts to give to family and friends: Potpourris, seasoning packets for soups, specially blended teas, salves, bath powder and bath bags. There is something very powerful about carefully blending and mixing these precious gifts from Mother Earth, knowing what their specific job is, the person for whom they are intended, and adding your own special wishes and love.

Another whole dimension of herbal lore is the making and use of flower essences. Flower essences are water-based solutions in which various flowers have been infused in a careful and ceremonial way to extract their healing properties. The difference here is that flower essences contain only minute amounts (if any) of the organic constituent of the flower; what they have absorbed is the energetic property of the flower. Therefore, their use in healing is found in their effect on the subtle bodies, particularly the emotional body. Many's the time I've administered Bach's Rescue Remedy to an hysterical child and watched its amazing calming effect take place within seconds. This whole subject was discovered and researched by a British medical doctor, Dr. Edward Bach, in the early years of this century.

There are some good books out on this subject (see Suggested Reading). My favorite is *Bach Flower Therapy* by Mechthild Scheffer. *Flower Essences and Vibrational Healing* by Gurudas gives instructions for making the essences.

If you are not interested in making them yourself, flower essences are obtainable at most natural food or herb stores.

In conclusion, I would like to share with you some practical information on the healing and ritual use of herbs from herbalist and author Michael Tierra.

In healing with herbs, many approaches are possible because herbs are truly the sacraments of the planet. Their healing properties can be used in many ways: as physical medicines in the form of special foods to alter the chemistry of the body and help it heal and maintain itself free from disease; as psychoactive agents that can engender specific states of consciousness upon the user, aiding self awareness; as magnets to attract and hold the energies of specific powers of the plant kingdom as well as the intentions of the healer-transmitter. As organic substances, plants attract and hold both subtle and gross material energy and can be simply carried and worn on the body as a talisman of healing.

In picking herbs in the wild (called in the trade "wildcrafting"), some basic considerations should be followed:

1) Harvest herbs in such a way as to not deplete or inhibit their future growth and development by taking only what you immediately need for yourself or those to whom you are going to administer them;

2) While never taking more than a third of the "stand" you are harvesting, always pick where there is abundant and luxuriant growth, as these herbs will possess the greatest healing potential;

3) Try to discover secret favorite areas for picking certain herbs away from the common highways and byways subject to pollution of traffic and the innocent harvesting by other herbalists;

4) Pick herbs at their therapeutical prime state—generally in the early morning (when the dew has just melted off the plant so as to prevent

their rotting) or in the afternoon (after the sun has passed its zenith and the plants have generally revived from the intense onslaught of midday heat. Leaves are harvested just before the flowering stage, flowers before the fruiting and seeding stage; most roots and barks are taken in the early spring or fall when the energies are concentrated in that part of the plant.

Many herbalists (including the great sixteenth century herbalist Nicolas Culpeper) attach astrological importance to the actual month and day that is optimum for harvesting individual herbs. Of course, this implies a knowledge of astrology and the assignment of planetary rulers to each plant species, which points up the cosmological interrelationship of plants to the celestial bodies and is a cornerstone of most systems of traditional herbology throughout the world.

What is of importance to the gatherer is the realization that each plant first exists as a channel of sun and moon energy as well as that of perhaps every star in the universe that influences the diversity of colors and forms of all plant life on this planet. The first job of plants is to nurture and heal Mother Earth and it is sad to consider that perhaps with the willful extinction by so-called human development of a plant species, Mother Earth herself is deprived of the nurturing and healing energies of her planetary and stellar community.

The use of amulets, talismans and charms integrating plants along with other substances from the animal and mineral kingdoms is part of all known folk traditions, as well as the very respected systems of traditional East Indian Ayurvedic medicine, middle eastern Unani medicine and traditional Chinese and Tibetan medicine. The Native Americans also had a very broad application of the concept of medicine which included standard herbal, dietary and physiotherapeutic treatments along with sacred charms, rituals, talismans, amulets, and sacred songs sung for special kinds of healing. In all cases, either the direct will and power of the medicine person was transferred to the patient via a plant talisman, for instance, to be worn in a special pouch, or the force of a well-established tradition empowered a seemingly innocuous plant substance with no significant physiological value into a talisman.

More often than not there is a solid scientific basis to so called "old wives' tales." Many folk traditions uphold the wearing of certain plants such as garlic, ginseng, and others to ward off evil spirits and contagion. The odor of plants is usually based upon the presence of certain volatile oils whose purpose is either to attract beneficial insects who would aid pollination or to repulse harmful pathogens. Certainly the odor of many of these plants, though often pleasant to our senses, seems to be repugnant to various bacteria. In its effort to protect itself from disease, the bruised plant inadvertently protects the wearer.

I don't intend to make light of the complex mystery involved in the use of talismans but rather to suggest that there is an empowerment of organic substances such as plants used in this way that extends from the known to the unknown, making them very useful in transpersonal healing.

How does a plant first acquire its therapeutic powers? Is it only through empirical discovery based on trial and error through countless ages of use, or could it also be that a single individual, through the will and force of his or her personality, literally empowers substances that will continue to possess genuine healing capacities that will be confirmed and transferred through generations? All of this seems to agree with the most modern concepts of quantum physics that theorizes that phenomena not only have intrinsic qualities but that what is observed is altered by the observer in the process of observation.

It seems that the most powerful intuitive state is achieved when our mind is generating alpha waves of from three to seven vibrations per second. My experience has shown me that alpha state is not even as deep as meditation because in alpha our ego is still seeming to be operable while in deep meditation all sense of personal ego is gone.

From all this, it would seem that the ideal purpose in making an herbal talisman is to create a ritual such as lighting a candle, fasting with a plant, meditating, drumming and chanting with it — any or all of which can be used to tap into the vital alpha consciousness that generates the energy of empowerment we are needing. Empowerment is the basis of the art of shamanism as it is with herbal healing. The alpha state, focussed on the object of our intention, is integral to all spiritual healing.

What is actually needed to make a talisman is comparatively of either little or great consequence depending on whether we are more or less an egoistically inclined shaman-healer. From past experiences I have found that neither good words, intentions nor even psychic powers, suggesting outer mastery, necessarily implies that one may be either a good person or, for that matter, has overcome personal limitation.

Of course, any plant can be used as a talisman that may have a special significance based upon where it is found, or various associations that will help focus our attention. The dimensions of herbal usage are as diverse as the infinite varieties of the plant kingdom itself. The limits are the boundaries of our creative imagination. The important thing in working with herbs is to revel in it. Let the process carry itself, and you, to whatever limitless expansion your heart can achieve.

PART 2

Ways of Celebration

CHAPTER 4

THE MAGIC OF HOME

The Path of the Hearthfire

Home. Just the very word conjures up for us many images, many feelings.

Home is where the heart is. Where is the heart? And what is the heart? What is the connection between heart and hearth?

Our hearts are the center of our being. On a physical level the heart is the centralized pump responsible for circulating blood throughout our bodies. Blood carries oxygen and nutrients. Thus our heart enables these life-giving substances to reach their faraway destinations within our bodies. On an energetic level the heart has to do with our ability to give and receive love—lifeblood of another sort.

We may use the word "heartstrings" to refer to our loving connections to others. Heartstrings are the energetic equivalent of the circulation system; they allow us to both give and receive the life-giving substance of love, circulating all of this energy through the constant movement of the heart chakra.

Similarly, a hearth is the center of a home. Traditionally, homes have included a fireplace of some sort, large or small, where meals were cooked and the family gathered for warmth, light and companionship during the darkness and cold. From this nurturing hearthplace the members of the family were enabled to go forth again into the world and to their daily tasks.

We frequently use analogies of fire when referring to our emotions, particularly love. The "fires of passion," hearts "aflame with love," are examples that spring to mind.

Both heart and hearth are central sources of warmth and life.

Though this modern era of central heating may have rendered the family fireplace obsolete in many instances, our homes (with or without fireplaces) are still our heart/hearth centers of warmth, light and life. They are our base of operations, our "center," our safe haven and refuge. They are places where we seek and find sustenance, both physically and metaphorically. They are not only places where we hang our hat, find a full pantry and have a warm bed, but places where we *live*—have experiences good and bad that feed us by causing us to grow; come to lick the wounds inflicted on us by the outside world; come to refresh ourselves and venture outward again. In this way, they make our lives in the outer world possible.

"There's no place like home" sighed a heartfelt Dorothy upon returning to her Kansas farm from Oz; and there wasn't a person watching the movie who did not know exactly what she meant.

As with other aspects of our lives, turning a mere house into a home can become, with consciousness, energy and ceremony, a wonderfully life-affirming spiritual experience.

Let us assume you have just purchased or rented a new dwelling and would like to really make the place your own. Of course the simple (or not so simple!) acts of scrubbing it thoroughly, repainting, moving in and setting up your furniture and possessions will go a long way towards making it look and feel like home. But how about preceding (or following) this with a ceremony that will take care of the energetic level of all this? Human emotion, as well as events that have occurred in the house, will have left their energetic imprint on the etheric levels (this is one of the causes of so-called "haunted houses"). This, as well as the physical dirt, needs to be cleaned.

In many ways, settling yourself into a new dwelling can be approached in the same way as any other ritual:

1) Clear the space of undesired energies

2) Bless and consecrate the space to its new purpose

3) Invoke help and protection from Spirit for whatever the undertaking is to be (in this case, living happily and healthily in your new dwelling).

The following ceremony can be used to cleanse and bless a home you are about to move into, or the one in which you are currently dwelling; modify this ceremony to your personal needs. I have used it both upon moving into a new dwelling and to help friends clear some outside and unfriendly influences from a place they had resided for many years. I hope this ceremony will be of assistance to you in cleansing and blessing the place of your heart/hearth:

FAMILY HOME BLESSING CEREMONY

This rite is best performed in a manner that will include not just the house but the entire property. In either case a patch of earth outside the house needs to be designated "Compost Heap."

Items necessary for this rite are a ceremonial (or simply new) broom, a candle within a secure candleholder, a small container of salt, a cup of water, a smudge stick or sage branch and matches. Some frankincense or a braid of sweetgrass are helpful additions.

Family and friends gather in the hearth center of the home (around a fireplace or wood stove is nice, but not essential). The ritual implements are laid out on an altar near this area. If there is no fireplace, choose a room in the house which feels like it will be the heart-center (sometimes this turns out to be the kitchen) and set up the altar in that room.

Let everyone join hands and link energies for a few moments in silence. Then the Lady of the House should explain to all present the purpose of the ceremony and how it is to be carried out, with parts of the ceremony assigned to the other members of the family.

When this has been accomplished, the ceremony begins:

(Though roles in this ritual have been assigned to Father and Mother, this is arbitrary. These roles may be filled by any family member who bears the appropriate energy.)

FATHER:
As we gather here to cleanse and bless this home,
We ask that the Spirit of this place, this land,
This unique spot upon Mother Earth,
Look with favor on our undertaking
And grant us help and blessings.

MOTHER:
Let us now call on the Guardians of the Four Directions to assist us.

EAST:
Guardians of the East, Powers of Air,
Place of the rising sun, we invite you to be with us now.
We ask the assistance of your cleansing breezes.
Greetings! You are welcome!

SOUTH:
Guardians of the South, Powers of Fire,
Place of the noonday sun, we invite you to be with us now.
We ask the assistance of your purifying fires.
Greetings! You are welcome!

WEST:
Guardians of the West, Powers of Water,
Place of the setting sun, we invite you to be with us now.

We ask the assistance of your diluting and dispersing waters.
Greetings! You are welcome!

NORTH:

Guardians of the North, Powers of Earth,
Place of the midnight sun, we invite you to be with us now.
We ask the assistance of your transmuting, composting earthiness.
Greetings! You are welcome!

Holding aloft each in turn, the elements are now blessed by the Mother and Father of the family.

MOTHER & FATHER:

Air, Fire, Water, Earth—
Elements and building blocks of our world—
We bless you, that you may aid us in this rite.

Three sprinkles of the salt are mixed into the cup of water. Then the elements are passed around and each person present is blessed with them by the person to his (or her) right. When this is complete the elements are set once again upon the altar.

MOTHER:

We invoke and call upon Thee, O Most Holy One,
Whom we affectionately call Father;

FATHER:

We invoke and call upon Thee, Wise and Compassionate One,
Whom we lovingly call Mother;

MOTHER & FATHER:

Lend us your aid for this rite of cleansing and blessing.

Now the Mother takes up the broom and goes to the farthest corner of the house. She begins sweeping, and goes through the entire house, sweeping out each room (closets and bathrooms included) from the back corners to the doorway.

MOTHER:

In the names of the Mother and the Father,
I sweep all that is old and outworn,
All that is evil and unnecessary,
Across this threshold and from this room.

When she has completed the sweeping of the entire house she sweeps the invisible pile of energy to the outside door closest to the designated Compost Heap area. Opening the door she sweeps the pile outside.

MOTHER:
> In the names of the Mother and the Father,
> I sweep all that is old and outworn,
> All that is evil and unnecessary,
> Across this threshold and from this house.

She sweeps the pile into the Compost Heap.

> Accept this offering, Mother Earth,
> Of energies in need of recycling.
> We offer them to you,
> That you may work your magic of transmutation upon them.
> Transform them, Mother, that they may become elements
> That will nourish future growth.
> Blessed be!

As Mother is sweeping, the person designated takes up the cup of salted water and follows her around the house, asperging room by room, sprinkling the consecrated water in the center of the room as well as around all of the room's boundaries, windows and doorways.

SALT WATER PERSON:
> I cleanse thee by water and earth.

The person designated follows with the sage, smudging the room.

SAGE PERSON:
> I cleanse and purify thee by fire and air.

The person designated follows with a lighted candle.

CANDLE PERSON:
> Let the light of spirit shine upon this work we have done.

The rest of the company present follows the person with the candle and holds within themselves the energy of cleansing and blessing, contributing in this manner to the work being done.

If desired, the sweeping and blessing can be continued outdoors, within the bounds of the property lines, before the final sweeping of it all to the Compost Heap.

When all has been swept into the heap, the broom is laid down near the heap and all turn to face the East. The members of the family, led by the oldest child and aided by the friends present, begin construction of a protective circle of energy around the house and property, walking the bounds of the property.

CHILD:
> By the power of God and Goddess,

We create around this, our home,
A circle of radiant light;
Guarding us, protecting us,
Allowing in only that which serves our highest good.
As we will, so mote it be!

Those bearing the elements follow and bless and consecrate the boundaries of the circle, adding their blessings in similar fashion. When this is done all return inside to the altar.

All join hands into a circle and Father, Mother or other adult family member speaks:

May this house be founded
On the goodness of the earth.
May the walls of this house be blessed
By the four winds of the heaven.
May the roof of this house be guarded
By the heights and the stars above.

So that all who live in this house,
All who seek shelter in this house,
All who strive, protected by this house,
Find hope and strength to live,
Find love and joy to give,
Find faith and meaning in their destiny.*

The Father now kindles either the frankincense or sweetgrass.

FATHER:
By Earth, by Water, by Fire, by Air—
And their combined power within this incense—
We ask that blessings flow to us,
Blow to us, take root in us, transform us.
Blessed be!

All smudge themselves with the incense, which is then carried from room to room throughout the house. When this has been done all return to the altar, where one of the younger children speaks.

CHILD:
Let us give thanks to those who have helped us.

---

*   Celtic origin

EAST:

> Spirits of the East, we give you thanks
> For your presence and your strength.
> We bid you farewell!

SOUTH:

> Spirits of the South, we give you thanks
> For your presence and your strength.
> We bid you farewell!

WEST:

> Spirits of the West, we give you thanks
> For your presence and your strength.
> We bid you farewell!

NORTH:

> Spirits of the North, we give you thanks
> For your presence and your strength.
> We bid you farewell!

MOTHER & FATHER:

> Mother and Father, Source of all being,
> We thank you for your presence and strength.
> We bid you farewell!

CHILD:

> Blessed be this place and this time,
> And those who are with us, seen and unseen.

ALL:

> Blessed Be!

CHAPTER 5

SAMHAIN

October 31st

Hey-ho for Halloween
When all the witches are to be seen,
Some in black and some in green,
Hey-ho for Halloween!
                    (Traditional)

I would like to begin this chapter with a piece by Ed Fitch and Janina Renee, telling about their family's Samhain (Hallowmas) observances:

* *

The popular Halloween festival has come to be very commercialized. Thus our family has chosen to balance things by concentrating on the more solemn aspects of this holiday, turning inward and dedicating ourselves to contemplation, study and renewal (similar to the Rosh Hashanah/Yom Kippur observances at this time of year). We feel that our children will get plenty of the Halloween festival gaiety at school and at their friends' houses.

Our family begins the Hallowmas observance on the evening of October 24th, the week prior to Halloween. If you haven't already put up Hallowmas decorations, this is a good time to do so. Halloween, as it has come to be practiced in our country, combines a number of elements: the agricultural harvest, the wild harvest, the transition of the fall foliage season into the onset of winter weather, and the commemoration of The Day of the Dead. All of these elements can be combined in your decor: autumn leaves; orange and yellow flowers; fruits, vegetables, and nuts; candles, lanterns, and luminaries lighting rooms, windows and garden pathways; jack-o'lanterns, black and orange crepe, costumes, and novelty items, etc. If your children want to include the more garish sort of commercial decorations these too have become an American tradition, and tradition is what it's all about!

If you have a little shrine or altar to honor your patron gods and spirits, include a little seasonal decoration here, too. Brighten it with autumn leaves and marigolds. Set out a small animal skull as a memento. Use black candles and a black velvet altar cloth, if you wish.

Because this is a special time for remembering our ancestors and our departed loved ones, and a solemn time set aside for contemplating the Mystery of Life and Death as taught by the ancient ways, we choose to begin our Hallowmas week on October 24th with a period of light fasting (simple, often meatless, sweetless and fatless meals). The fasting comes to an end with the early supper and Halloween treats on the evening of the 31st. We also try to avoid going out or engaging in too many social activities during Hallowmas week, because this is a time which families should spend together, sharing knowledge of the past. We set aside a special area for each night's commemoration. The area should be quiet and comfortable, large enough for the family to gather in a circle to listen to stories and practice divination. A candle or hearth fire should serve as a focal point. A white candle could be used as a symbol of the Divine or a black candle as a symbol of the mysteries of death and the afterlife. (The candle should be replaced and relit each evening—this is a good job for one of the children). If you have a favorite form of divination—tarot cards, I Ching, crystal ball, etc.—a table (or the hearth) should be prepared for this, also occupying a central position.

Our family also keeps its own chest of ancestor relics, personal belongings of now-departed family members (such as Grandpa's scarf or Grandma's fan). During the week we bring out these various relics, as well as old family albums; we look over all the various photos and mementos, recounting the life histories of those represented.

We tend to dedicate each night of Hallowmas to a special subject; one night we may dedicate to ghost stories (which can be instructive in dealing with theories of life and death), another to the heroic myths of ancient times, another evening to legends of the fairy folk, and so on. We may also choose to focus on different ancestors each night, perhaps one evening recounting the lives of ancestors who heroically served their countries, another telling about those of our people who have been martyred for their faith, their convictions, or freedom, and perhaps another evening set aside for those ancestors who were dedicated to the various arts, as well as an evening to remember family pets.

A Family Fire Festival is held on All-Hallows Eve. On the big night of October 31st, after routine trick or treat festivities are completed, we have a simple family fire festival, rekindling the hearthfire, and also the pilot lights in our home, in honor of this ancient season of renewal. A great deal of importance is made of this rekindling, which is done by the children. Much mention is also made that Samhain is the Herald of Winter. Candles are set in the windows, and the doors are unlocked. The meal is served at midnight, with the dead invited to join with the family. (A plate of food is set out for the dead; the physical food is given to family pets afterwards.) Prayers are said for the recent dead and, insofar as is known, the favorite foods of departed relatives is served. If fellow Pagan families are visiting, this meal may be a big potluck. Prayers are offered especially for the martyrs and for the souls which must undergo their own purgatories.

THE SOUL NIGHTS OF ALL-HALLOWS WEEK

October 24th—Festival prelude and Night of the Seers—Children put up seasonal decorations, parents set up family shrine then spend time remembering ancestors and other historical figures who have dealt with the supernatural or who have foreseen the future.

October 25th—The Night of the Heroes and Martyrs—Remembering those members of the family who have done much in war and in peace, including those who have died for their faith, their convictions, or for freedom, and recounting their deeds.

October 26th—The Night of the Artists—Remembering those who have spoken of the Old Ways, through art, music or literature, and whose work evokes magic.

October 27th—The Night of the Nurturers—Remembering those family members who have nurtured and preserved; those who have kept the home fires burning; those who persevered in fulfilling the difficult job of taking care of those who were in need of care.

October 28th—The Night of Remembrance for Family Pets—Pets are family members, and must be recalled and their memories cherished.

October 29th—The Night of Remembrance of Forgotten Ancestors—Discuss what you do know about your ancestors, and speculate on what their lives must have been like. Reach farther into the past and speculate on even more distant ancestors and family heritage and origins.

October 30th—The Night of the Recent Dead—Plan a trip to the cemetery earlier in the day, if possible. Spend the evening remembering relatives and friends, looking at pictures of them, handling their personal belongings, and telling about their lives.

October 31st—Family Fire Festival—This is a night to honor all the departed souls. After mundane celebration, a prayer ceremony is held for souls undergoing purification. Relighting of hearth fire, pilot lights. Welcoming of the dead to a commemorative midnight dinner.

RITUAL FORMAT FOR THE SOUL NIGHTS

Needed: candles, lanterns, table, mementos, divination tools, bell. All gather together in the selected area. The hearthfire, lanterns and candles are lit. Each child may select a favorite Halloween candle to be lit. All artificial lights are put out.

A bell is provided, to be rung by one of the children (in the evenings that follow a different child may take a turn each night). As the family stands in a circle around the central candle (or half-circle around the hearth) holding hands, the bell-ringer steps forward. He or she rings the bell three times to banish all unwelcome spirits and welcome the good. Then one or all may recite:

We banish from this place all spirits who would cause us harm.
We welcome to this place all spirits who would bring us benefit.
Blessed Be.

At this point all sit down and the adults alternate in recalling departed loved ones or reading appropriate stories and legends.

After the storytelling session it is desirable to request a message from the spirits. To do this, prepare whatever form of divination you favor, then one or all should recite:

Weave around us, Great Mother, a circle of radiant light,
Allowing in only that which is of service to us.
Blessed Be.

Now proceed with the divination. Frame your questions: "Is there a special message from those departed souls we have talked about tonight?" Interpretations should be made using the evening's topic as the prime frame of reference.

When it is time to bring the session to an end, one or all should recite:

Unseen friends,
We thank you for your help, guidance and inspiration,
And as you depart we bid you farewell.
Blessed Be.

The bell is rung again three times and the evening's ceremony is complete.

PRACTICAL SUGGESTIONS

Children always enjoy decorating the house for Halloween.

Visit graves and cemeteries.

In family reading and narrations, discuss the meaning of Halloween from a Pagan point of view.

Children and parents can make lanterns together to put in windows and to hang in trees.

Take a special nature outing, enjoy the seasonal colors (if you are lucky enough to have them in your locale). Visit one of your favorite natural magical sites.

Go to a pumpkin patch and select your Halloween pumpkins.

Seasonal songs can be sung together.

A vigil light can be kept in the seasonal shrine, burning day and night, for the duration of the festival.

This is an appropriate time for housecleaning and closet cleaning, to get rid of that which is outworn.

The table each night can be set with seasonal plates, cups, napkins, etc. and decorated with symbols of the season.

Each child can pick out a Halloween candle, which can be lit before dinner and kept burning during the meal or until bedtime.

On the night of the Fire Festival a bell can be rung to summon the spirits of the dead to the meal.

Dinner can be by candlelight each night of this week.

* * * * * * * * * * * * * * * * * * * *

We feel the energy of Samhain is not confined to one night, October 31st, but actually stretches for about five or six days, sometimes longer. We feel the energy building up, peaking, then slowly fading away. We try to go with this flow in our family celebration.

In our family's Samhain celebration we have adopted as much of the suggestions from our friends Ed Fitch and Janina Renee as seems to fit our family. Early evening on the night of Samhain usually finds us quite busy. Trick or treaters begin knocking at the door shortly before dark and our kids take turns answering and doling out the treats. Of course our house is appropriately and spookily decorated and sometimes even Mom and Dad are in costume. The table has a Halloween tablecloth on it, and while Mom cooks the traditional meal of Bubble and Squeak, children set the table making sure to include an extra place setting for the spirits. The candles and jack-o'lanterns are lit and the artificial lights turned off or down. A candle is placed in the front window to welcome home the spirits. The dinner is placed upon the table in cast iron pots to keep it warm during the ritual. The children choose which quarter they would like to call in and the ritual begins (ritual is below). Following the ritual the meal is eaten in silence. After the meal the children take the dish of food for the spirits and leave it outside on the porch, then they hurry into their Halloween costumes. For the next two or three hours trick-or-treating or a Halloween festival at school is enjoyed by all.

When we return home all children are readied for bed, reminding them that the spirits of the dead will be about tonight. We stress to them that they are safe and protected, that tonight is the night they might feel the loving spirit of Great Grandma or Uncle George. The children's personal jack-o'lanterns are brought into their bedrooms and lit, prayers are said, and they are tucked into their beds. After the children are asleep the jack-o'lantern candles are extinguished for safety reasons.

The next day, November 1st, being the day of Samhain, we continue the in the "spirit" of the previous night by telling ghost stories (true ones, of course!) or recounting any special dreams of the previous night. At night we light our jack-o'lanterns again. We do this each night until the jack-o'lanterns need to be composted. Since we saved seeds for spring planting from the pumpkins while they were being carved, this makes the lesson complete.

ACTIVITIES

There are many traditional Halloween games. Most of them involve apples, nuts and fire, these elements being very symbolic of the season. In many places, this is the time of the apple harvest, so apples are plentiful. Nuts are also ready to harvest, and, as our friends the squirrels know, store very well throughout the cold months. Fire, of course, represents not only the power of light keeping the cold darkness at bay, but the power of the undying light of Spirit. In some areas of Britain, Halloween is known as Nutcrack Night or Apple and Candle Night.

One of the most familiar Halloween activities is ducking or bobbing for apples. A quantity of apples is placed in a large tub and people, kneeling, attempt to capture an apple using their mouths instead of their hands, which are tied behind their backs. Sometimes an apple is hung down from the ceiling with a length of string, gently set swinging, and the person must try to catch and eat it without using his hands.

Divination games have always been popular on this "night of the thin veil". To discover the name of a future mate, an apple is peeled carefully, so that the peel comes off in one, long strip. The peel is then (or even better, at the stroke of midnight) tossed over the enquirer's left shoulder and the initial of the future lover can be read from the shape taken by the peel as it lies on the floor.

Another divination game concerning future spouses required the person to stand before a mirror eating an apple and, at the same time, combing the hair. This is done by candlelight. The form of the future spouse will appear in the mirror, looking over the person's left shoulder. Yet another game involves placing two nuts on the bars of the fireplace grate, or in the embers. One of the nuts is named for a young woman, the other for a young man. If they burn quietly together the couple will marry, but if they flare up or explode or pop away from each other the couple's romance is doomed.

Sometimes a wish was written on a piece of paper which was rolled up and thrown into the hearth fire. If it burned away quickly and completely the wish would come true. Bonfires were traditional on this night, lit at dusk. They were for protection against any evil spirits who might be roaming the world this night, as well as for blessing of the fields, for luck, for merriment, and for just plain fun. The people danced around them, leaped through the flames or over the embers. Bonfires, like jack-o'lanterns, represented the protection given by light over the dark coldness of the coming winter.

Autumn's bountiful offerings to us can be used in craft activities with children. Here are some ideas.

1) Acorns, with their jaunty little caps, can be dried, then drilled and strung into necklaces (as can dried rosehips).

2) Other nuts of varying sizes and shapes can be glued together, given faces with a felt tip pen, and costumed.

3) Apples (or pears, potatoes, etc.) can be held together with toothpicks or sharpened sticks driven through them to create apple people. A wad of modeling clay on the bottom can be fashioned into feet to hold up the apple person. Two shorter sharpened sticks can serve as arms. Sewing pins can be used to fasten berries or raisins to the top apples, thus creating a face. These can then be costumed with bits of old felt or fabric.

4) Dried Indian corn can be bound together by the leaves with twine or a colorful ribbon to create a front door decoration.

5) Green or autumn-colored leaves can be tied with colored yarn in various places to create leaf people, with twigs inserted for arms.

6) Fallen twigs and small branches can be decorated with yarn and feathers in a prayerful manner to create prayer arrows.

7) Besides the usual pumpkin jack-o'lanterns, other vegetables such as turnips, rutabagas, or even melons, can be hollowed out and faces carved. Put in an appropriate sized candle and you have a jack-o'lantern with a difference! Try making several of these lanterns, varying the vegetable used and the facial expressions, to light a path to your front door for the trick-or-treaters.

8) Ornamental gourds can be dried, then gently sanded with steel wool to remove their waxy outer layer. To open them puncture one spot with a sharp object, then continue sawing with a fine toothed saw. Once open, remove pulp and seeds, clean thoroughly, then use steel wool to clean and polish the insides. They can then be decorated to become bowls, dippers, scoops, vases or anything else your imagination conjures up. If they are to hold food or liquid coat the inside surface with a thin layer of beeswax for waterproofing.

9) Gourds can also be used to make ceremonial rattles. When they are completely dried (and this could take quite a while) drill a small hole in one end and use tweezers (or a similar tool) to extract the dried pulp and seeds. When the gourd is empty, insert a few small beans as noise makers. Then glue a wooden stick to the opening to seal it and act as a handle for your rattle. The rattles can be individualized as ceremonial objects by painting them with sacred symbols; they can then be decorated by tying feathers onto them. The sound of a rattle has the ability to alter consciousness. Rattles are also used to call the spirits, to get their attention when we communicate with them, an appropriate activity during this Samhain season.

RECIPES

BUBBLE AND SQUEAK

Bubble and Squeak is an Irish dish traditionally eaten on Hallowmas. It gets its name from the sounds the vegetables make while they are cooking. The sounds are reputed to frighten away any evil spirits.

1 large potato for everyone (including your spirit guests)
1 medium to large head of green cabbage
2 medium onions
2-3 cloves of garlic
butter, margarine and/or cooking oil
salt, pepper

Cube the potatoes and boil them until tender. Chop the cabbage into fairly small pieces and boil until soft. Chop the onions and garlic and saute them until translucent.

In a large bowl, combine the potatoes, cabbage, onions and garlic. Season to taste with the salt and pepper.

In a large cast iron skillet or griddle, heat the butter, margarine or oil until very hot and spoon in a large dollop of the potato-cabbage mixture. Spread it out on the bottom of the skillet with a spatula. It should be like a large pancake and about 1/4 - 1/2 inch thick. Fry thoroughly on each side.

BOXTY

Boxty is an Irish dish eaten at Hallowmas (as well as other holiday occasions). It is a potato pancake, but more breadlike than Bubble and Squeak due to the omission of cabage and the addition of flour.

4 cups potatoes, peeled and grated (about 2 pounds)
1 1/3 cups flour
2 teaspoons salt
1/2 cups brown sugar
4 tablespoons melted butter

Squeeze the potatoes as dry as possible using a tea towel or paper towel. Combine the flour, salt and potatoes in a bowl. Stir the milk in gradually, using just enough to make the mixture hold together. Let stand for 1 hour. Heat a ten inch skillet until very hot. Melt the butter in it. Using a spatula, pat the potato mixture into the skillet evenly. Cook over medium flame until the underside is set and golden brown. To brown the other side, slide pancake out onto a plate and invert the plate so the pancake falls gently back into the skillet. Serve the pancake hot with melted butter and sprinkle with brown sugar. Serves six.

PARKIN CAKE

Parkin Cake is served in England on Guy Fawkes Day, November 5th. On this date in 1604 Guy Fawkes tried to blow up King James I of England and his Parliament. This unsuccessful event became known as the Gunpowder Plot. The commemoration of this event gradually became merged with the older Samhain fire festival in the minds of the people. There were huge bonfires on November 5th, and burnings in effigy, marking the idea of a struggle between darkness and light. This cake is both sweet and spicy. It is sometimes called a Thar or Thor Cake, pointing to possible Saxon origins. In some parts of England Guy Fawkes is completely forgotten and November 5th is referred to as Parkin Day.

1/2 cup butter
2/3 cup light molasses
2/3 cup rolled oats
1 cup flour
1 tablespoon sugar
1/2 teaspoon ginger

1/4 teaspoon cloves
1/2 teaspoon salt
1/2 teaspoon baking powder
1 teaspoon lemon rind (optional)
1/2 cup milk

Combine the dry ingredients by sifting together. Melt the butter and gradually mix in the molasses.

Add the butter mixture, alternately with the milk, to the dry ingredients, combining until everything is just moist. The batter will be thin. Pour into a greased cake pan and bake in a preheated 350 degree oven for 30-35 minutes.

LAMB'S WOOL

The apple is an integral part of autumnal lore in the British tradition. Apples ripen in the fall and are delicious and plentiful. These beautiful fruits, whose fragrant blossoms at Beltane betoken the sweet abundance of summer, at Samhain become symbolic of the passage into the darker realms of the year.

This apple beverage came to us from the Druids and was originally called "La Mas Ushal." The traditional way to make it was to put a container filled with spiced ale or cider in front of a blazing log. Above it apples were hung on strings to roast until the well-cooked pulp fell in little puffy heaps into the cider. The following recipe is an easier way to do it.

2 gallons mulled ale
2 eggs
5 apples
5 pinches of nutmeg
3 or 4 pounds of honey
a handful of browned toast

Pour ale into a large bowl and beat in the eggs. Add nutmeg and let set for a few hours in a cool place (the refrigerator is not a bad idea; food poisoning from contaminated raw eggs is not a pleasant experience). Dice the apples, put into a saucepan with a little water or cider and cook at low heat until soft. Mix the honey with the cooked apples and let set for a while, stirring occasionally. Add the apple mixture to the ale mixture and mix well. Serve heated with the toast floating on top.

If you prefer to make a nonalcoholic version of this use apple cider instead of the ale. It won't be the same but will still be good and much better for the children.

SOUL CAKES

"A soul, a soul, a soul cake. Please dear Missus, a soul cake..." goes the old song. The custom of souling was observed at this time of year in the British Isles. Visitors on or around the feast of All Souls (November 2nd) were given soul cakes. (Halloween, also called All Hallows Eve, or All Saints Eve, is October 31st. All Saints Day is November 1st and All Souls Day is November 2nd.) Even today children in some parts of England still go souling; they wander from house to house singing and collecting bits of food or some money, ostensibly for the souls of the dead who are said to return to their former homes at this time of year. This custom developed into the American trick-or-treating tradition.

7-8 cups flour
1 teaspoon salt
1 cup softened butter
1/2 cup honey
1 tablespoon yeast
2 eggs
1 teaspoon allspice
milk

Mix the flour, salt and allspice together. Work in the softened butter with your fingers or cut it in with two knives until it is in tiny crumblike pieces. Mix the yeast into about 1/4 cup warm milk and 1 teaspoon of the honey. Let sit for a few minutes. Add the eggs and 1/2 cup warm milk to the yeast mixture and stir. Add the liquids to the dry ingredients, adding enough warm milk to form a soft dough. Let rise for about 1/2 an hour. Then form the dough into round, flat rolls and let rise for an additional 15 minutes. Bake at 425 degrees for 15 minutes.

PUMPKIN OATMEAL COOKIES

The cheerful orange pumpkins, now traditional at Halloween, are to me reminiscent of the golden-orange glow of the setting sun.

1/2 cup softened butter
1 cup brown sugar or 1/2 cup honey
2 eggs
1 teaspoon vanilla
1 cup pureed pumpkin
1 1/2 cups flour (whole wheat pastry flour or unbleached)
1 1/2 cups oatmeal (grind rolled oats in a blender, but not into a flour)
1/2 teaspoon baking soda
1/2 teaspoon salt
1 teaspoon cinnamon
1/4 teaspoon nutmeg
1/4 teaspoon cloves
1/2 cup raisins
1/2 cup chopped walnuts or pecans

Cream together butter and sugar (or honey). Beat in eggs. Mix in pumpkin and vanilla. In a separate bowl, mix together flour, oatmeal, salt, soda and spices. Add to the pumpkin mixture. Stir in raisins and nuts. Drop by teaspoonful onto a baking sheet and bake at 375 degrees for 12 minutes.

PUMPKIN SOUP

1 thinly sliced onion

2 tablespoons oil
2 cups pureed pumpkin
2 cups chicken broth (vegetarian chicken-flavored broth
    powder is available in natural food stores)
2 tablespoon cornstarch
1 teaspoon salt
2 cups milk (soymilk can be used)
1/4 teaspoon marjoram
1/4 teaspoon ginger
dash of pepper
sprinkles of cinnamon
hollowed out pumpkin shell

In a large soup pot, saute the onion in the oil. In a separate bowl, mix together the salt, the pumpkin and 1 1/2 cups of the chicken broth. Add to the soup pot and bring to a boil. Turn immediately down to a simmer and allow ingredients to simmer for 10 minutes. Add the seasonings and milk. Heat through. Stir together the cornstarch and the remaining 1/2 cup of chicken broth. Add to soup and stir until soup thickens slightly. Pour soup into a hollowed out pumpkin shell. Dish into bowls and sprinkle each serving with a dash of cinnamon.

STUFFED PUMPKIN

2 cups uncooked rice (brown or white)
4 cups water
1 teaspoon salt
5 cloves minced garlic
1 large onion, chopped
2 tablespoon oil
4 carrots, chopped into rounds, steamed
1/4 pound mushrooms, thickly sliced, sauteed
1 large or 2 small zucchini, sliced, sauteed
4 tablespoons toasted sunflower seeds
2 teaspoons toasted sesame seeds
2 cups cooked garbanzo beans
2-3 tablespoons soy sauce
1-2 tablespoons Worcestershire sauce
1/2-3/4 cup finely grated parmesan (optional)
1 tsp dried basil
1/2 teaspoon dried oregano
1 3 to 4 pound pumpkin, seeds and pulp removed

In a large pot with a tight fitting lid, heat the oil and saute the onion and garlic until soft and translucent. Add 4 cups of water, 1 teaspoon salt and bring to a boil. Add rice, bring again to a boil, cover, turn down to a simmer and cook until done (45 minutes for brown rice, 15-20 minutes for white rice). While rice is cooking, chop and steam carrots and zucchini until somewhat soft. Toast sunflower and sesame seeds (separately) in a dry, heated frying pan. (Heat them until they begin to smell toasty and get brown, turning frequently.) Cook garbanzos by your usual method (or buy canned). Put vegetables, seeds, beans and rice into a large bowl. Add seasonings, soy sauce, Worcestershire sauce and cheese. Stir carefully so as not to mash the rice.

Rub the inside of the pumpkin with a mixture of soy and Worcestershire sauce and spoon in the rice mixture. Cook in a preheated 375 degree oven until pumpkin is done (about 1 1/2 hours). If you wish you can precook the pumpkin. Simply put it, hollowed out, in a preheated oven for 1/2 hour or so until not quite so hard. Then fill it with the rice mixture and continue cooking until done.

PUMPKIN BREAD

1 cup pureed pumpkin
3/4 cup honey
1/3 cup oil
2 eggs
1 3/4 cups whole wheat pastry flour (or
    use 1 cup whole wheat and 3/4 cup unbleached flours)
2 teaspoons baking powder
1 1/3 teaspoons cloves
1/2 teaspoon cinnamon
scant 1/4 teaspoon salt
2-3 tablespoons water
3/4 cup walnuts or pecans, chopped
3/4 cup raisins

Mix together oil, eggs, honey and pumpkin. Slowly add dry ingredients, using the water if the batter seems too dry. Stir in nuts and raisins. Spoon batter into a bread pan and bake one hour in a 350 degree preheated oven. Allow to cool for several minutes before turning loaf out onto a plate to continue cooling. Do not attempt to slice until loaf is completely cool.

WHEAT GERM COOKIES

7 tablespoons butter or margarine
2 tablespoons brown sugar (packed)
3/4 cup wheat germ
3/4 cup whole wheat pastry flour
1/2 teaspoon salt
2 hard-cooked egg yolks, grated
3 tablespoon milk
Cinnamon topping:
1 tablespoon wheat germ
2 tablespoons brown sugar
1/2 teaspoon cinnamon

Reserve 1 tablespoon butter. Beat 6 tablespoons of the butter with the sugar until well blended. Mix in flour, salt, wheat germ, and egg yolks. Blend in the milk to form a dough. Roll out on a floured surface to 1/4 - 1/2 inch thickness. Cut with Halloween (or animal) shaped cookie cutters. Brush tops with reserved butter, melted. Top with the cinnamon topping and place on an ungreased baking sheet. Bake at 350 degrees for 12 minutes or until lightly browned. Remove immediately from baking sheet.

BLACK CAT PUNCH

Mix sparkling or mineral water with grape juice, to taste.

FAMILY SAMHAIN RITUAL

This ritual was written by our good friend JoAnn Adams for an extended family Samhain many years ago. Now it has become a treasured part of our yearly cycle whether we do it circling a cauldron or sitting at the dinner table.

Needed: lots of candles, cauldron with desserts in it, god and goddess images, votive candles for all.

(Obviously this needs to be modified if done at the dinner table.)

After a short period of meditation, the children begin to circle slowly around the cauldron and the person assigned to each quarter lights the candle and invokes:

EAST:

    Guardians of the East,
    Elementals of Air,
    Circle round with us here
    Whispering the names of our loved ones,
    Giving passage to their spirits between the worlds.

SOUTH:

    Guardians of the South,
    Elementals of Fire,
    Circle round with us here,
    Warming us with your presence,
    Giving passage to our loved ones between the worlds.

WEST:

    Guardians of the West,
    Elementals of Water,
    Circle round with us here,
    Riding smoothly across the Western Sea from Summerland,
    Giving passage to our loved ones between the worlds.

NORTH:

    Guardians of the North,

Elementals of Earth,
Circle round with us here,
Strengthening the bonds of love between us,
Giving passage to our loved ones between the worlds.

All be seated if not already so.

PRIEST:

The Reaper comes among us at this time of the year, swinging his
black scythe—the harvest is upon us. The bounty of the summer season is stored in the granaries of the tribe to sustain us throughout
the dark days ahead. And as the Reaper passes, harvesting both the
essence of the grain and the souls of the Lady's people, he also
rends the veil that separates the living from the dead, the Land of
Home from Summerland. At this time we are reunited with those
who have passed into Summerland to learn again the lesson that life
and death come equally to all and are separated by the merest of
illusions. That as they are, so we have been, and will be again, and
that they shall be again as we are now; over and over as we spiral upward, dancing our way back to the presence of the Great Mother,
even as the smoke and ash of the fires of autumn dance their way
upward into the starlit sky.

*Pause for a few minutes of silent meditation. The hearthfire is lit by the man
of the house.*

PRIESTESS:

We do summon, stir and call thee forth,
Ye ancient mighty dead.
Give us of your wisdom, you who have dwelt on Mid-Earth, who are
sages of the Old Ways.
We welcome you to be here with us;
To warm yourselves at our hearthfire
And to know the love that glows within this sacred circle.
Share your wisdom, illuminate our hearts,
And show us the greater cycle of our lives;
That through you we may know that life never ends,
But only changes form.

Short pause.

Let us each light a candle in the name of those who have gone before us, remembering that in the midst of death there is life, light in
the midst of darkness, sunrise after sunset, and that spring must inevitably follow winter.

Everyone lights a candle, puts it by their plate, or on the hearth, and if they choose, dedicate it to a departed friend or relative.

PRIEST AND PRIESTESS:

Family and friends and guests unseen, as we partake of this food, fruits of the harvest, we ask you to join us as we celebrate the closing of this harvest season and the beginning of a New Year.

Happy New Year and Blessed Be!

MUSIC

SOUL CAKE

traditional

A   soul   a   soul   a   soul   cake,   please good mis-sus a soul cake, an

ap-ple   a   pear   or plum   or   a   cher-ry   or   a - ny good thing to make us mer-ry.

One   for   Pet - er   two   for   Paul,   three   for   him   who made us   all.

JACK-O'LANTERN

Lois Holt

1. Jack-O - lan - tern, Jack-O - lan - tern, You are such a pret-ty sight. As you
2. You were once a yel-low pump - kin, Grow-ing on a stur-dy vine, Now you

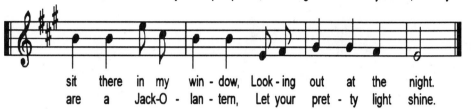

sit there in my win - dow, Look-ing out at the night.
are a Jack-O - lan - tern, Let your pret - ty light shine.

Dark Mother (Poem)
by Margie McArthur

Dark Mother who rides the night sky
On winds of change to the deep of winter;
You guide souls of loved ones to Summerland's rest,
To await rebirth among loved ones.

Ancestors will visit this night,
Guided home by the light in the window.
Warmed by our fires and cheered by our love;
The circle of life is unending.

Lord of Life and Lord of Death;
You are the Comforter and the Consoler.
In the midst of your dark nights we remember your dawn
The circle of love is unending.

CHAPTER 6

YULE

Winter Solstice - December 21st

The Holly bears a prickle
As sharp as any thorn,
And the Mother bore the Holy Child
On Solstice Day in the morn.

There is much that can be done to celebrate Yule. Many of the customs and songs surrounding Christmas are pagan in origin, so may be retained and slightly modified. Since Christmas is the time the Christians celebrate the birth of God the Son, and Pagans celebrate the birth of God the Sun, it is a good time for ecumenism.

In our family, we use Advent calendars and crèches as well as the more pagan Yule log and mistletoe. We make it a time of talking about the yearly cycle, the wheel of the year and the birth of the sun (we use as many of the legends about the births of various sun gods as we can find). We make it a time of activity: decorating the house, making gifts, making tree ornaments, baking, singing.

Each year I make up a large, decorated poster in the style of an advent calendar with 25 doors on it. (Advent is a term referring to the four weeks preceding Christmas but the word translates from the Latin as simply "arrival.") Behind each door is a special activity to be done on that day to prepare for the holiday. If your family celebrates Christmas make the poster with 25 doors, if you do not, then make it with 21 or 22 doors (to correspond with the date of Yule). The activities can include things like baking cookies and mailing them to out of area friends, putting up certain, special decorations (I thought of this one to keep the decorations from all going up on one day, to stretch it out a little), Yule and or Christmas caroling (just for your own enjoyment or in the community to brighten the day of shut-ins and senior citizens), bringing in the Yule log, making presents, and celebrating certain special days that fall within this period and are related to winter themes.

The first of these days is St. Nicholas Day, December 6th. St. Nicholas, besides his well known Christian associations, is also related to Odin or Woden, who was referred to as Old Nic, and who went about in a cape and a wide-brimmed hat, riding on his white horse as some depictions of St. Nicholas still show.

For St. Nicholas Day, we have tea and Speculaas cookies and at night we all put out our shoes to see if we've been good enough all year to warrant treats from the good saint/god. Those whose behavior has been less than exemplary during the year frequently do an "on the spot repentance" lest they find a lump of coal (or modern equivalent thereof) in their shoe in the morning. Many promises of good behavior are usually made on this night.

Another special day is St. Lucia's Day, December 13th, a Swedish celebration rooted in the winter solstice observance, later Christianized around an early Christian saint, Lucia, who was of Sicilian origin. Missionaries brought her story to Sweden and it somehow took root. The word Lucia comes from the Latin *lux,* meaning 'light.' This leads me to believe that the good saint Lucia is really a sun goddess in a Christian disguise.

We have adapted the traditional Swedish customs of Lucia Day within our family's observance of this occasion. Our daughters take turns being the Lucia Queen—greeting us early on the morning of December 13th carrying a tray of special rolls and coffee or hot chocolate. The Lucia Queen is clothed in a white robe and wears a crown of candles on her head. Sometimes instead of a candle crown (which worries me with the younger ones) a taper or votive candle is carried on the tray of goodies. Although there is a song that goes with this ceremony, I have been unable to obtain it, so I wrote a poem that our Lucia Queen recites as she delivers the morning treats.

Bringing in the Yule log can be a fun family observance. In times of old, it was one of the most important features of Christmas festivities in many parts of Europe. The Yule log was the bonfire of spring, summer and fall brought indoors. All the same virtues were ascribed to it: fertility, purification, continuation of life, protection from evil and such.

Much ritual and ceremony surrounded the bringing home and kindling of the Yule log. The log was of oak, ash or fruit wood. Usually it was considered unlucky to purchase the log. It had to be cut from one's own property, or failing that, someone else's. It could be a gift from someone, but money could not be exchanged for it. It was decorated with evergreen boughs and brought home in a horse or oxen-drawn cart and was ceremonially brought into the house and laid upon the open hearth. It was kindled with a piece of the last year's log that had been saved for the purpose. Sometimes it was sprinkled with corn and cider before being lit. Once lit, it was essential that it burn steadily until the time came for it to be extinguished. In some areas it was the custom to burn it for twelve hours; in other areas, for the entire twelve days of Christmas. Either way, it was never allowed to burn away completely, an event that would have presaged bad luck in the coming year. It was quenched at the appropriate time, making sure a fragment was saved to kindle the fire for the following year. In Cornwall, the figure of a man was drawn upon it, to char and fade in the fire and smoke as the log smoldered through the season. (Since the opposite sabbat, Litha, concerns the battle between the twin Sun Gods/Kings of the light and dark halves of the year, this image of the man drawn and allowed to char and fade on the Yule log might possibly be a Winter Solstice echo of the death aspect of this myth.)

In other parts of Europe there was even more ceremony. The Log was adorned with flowers, leaves and bits of colorful ribbon or fabric. While it was being brought home, songs were sung invoking fertility in women, crops, herds and flocks. The Log was brought into the house at dusk with great ritual and the doorway through which it passed was decorated with candles on either side. Corn and wine were poured over it as it passed across the threshold. The oldest man of the family laid it on the fire, and said prayers for the welfare of every living creature of the home and farm. The ashes from the Log were used for healing, protection and fertility. Sometimes they were scattered over the fields to grant fertility or into wells to keep the water pure.

The old custom of wassailing is worth reviving. The word 'wassail' is derived from the Anglo-Saxon 'waes hael' meaning 'be whole' or 'be of good health.' To wassail a person was to drink to his or her health and prosperity in a ceremonial way. At Yuletide a large bowl filled with a hot spiced ale drink containing toast (usually Lamb's Wool or variants thereof) was passed around in much the same manner as a loving cup. If the bowl was too large to be passed around, individual cups were filled from it. The master of the house was the first to drink, followed by the mistress, and so on through the rest of the family, and then the guests. Sometimes wassailing bowls were carried around, house to house, and songs were sung by those bringing the bowl. The songs were usually toasts to the health of the inhabitants of the house as well as a request for a small nip of the ale. The bowls were usually made of wood, and decorated with colored ribbons.

In the fruit growing districts of Britain, the apple orchards were wassailed during the Christmas/Yule season, usually at Twelfth Night (see below). The farmers, their families and their workers went to the orchard after dark bearing horns, guns (in more recent times) and a large pail of cider. The best tree in the orchard was chosen to represent all of the trees. Cider was poured around its roots, a piece of toast was laid in its fork and the lowest branches were pulled down and dipped in the cider pail, if possible. The tree was toasted, its health was drunk (thus acknowledging it as a conscious entity, worthy of respect) and a special, traditional song was sung to it. This done, shots were fired, horns were blown, or lacking these, buckets were beaten upon. All this commotion was to drive away the evil spirits and to awaken the sleeping trees. This ceremony was done to protect the orchards from harm (from unfriendly spirits and other evil influences) and to encourage them to bear a plentiful crop in the season to come. Songs for this are given below.

The modern custom of the Christmas tree became popular in Germany in the sixteenth century and was introduced to the United States in the nineteenth century, but the roots of this custom go well back in time.

In ancient Scandinavia and Britain, trees (probably oak) were decorated with gilded apples and lighted candles to honor Odin and Baldur. In later times, the evergreen, whose green branches in winter symbolized eternal life, became the tree venerated during this season. In ancient Rome, the winter solstice feast of Saturnalia was observed with much generosity and exchange of gifts. Laurel and pine boughs were brought in and decorated with trinkets.

The most likely primogenitor of our beloved Christmas Tree is the ancient World-Tree, an archaic and consistent theme found in many lands around the globe.

The World-Tree, whose branches reached to the Upperworlds, whose roots were anchored in the Underworld and whose trunk represented this world of Middle Earth, plays a large part in the Celto-Germanic mythos from which our western culture claims its heritage. The World-Tree is a potent symbol that unites all the worlds and all the dimensions. It is the means by which one moves from one dimension to the next, ascending or descending the tree in a shamanic sense. It is a reminder of our interconnectedness with all levels of being.

And so at the winter solstice, when all is dark and cold, and the world of nature seems asleep or dead, we gaze upon the evergreen tree and remember immortality. We think of its strong roots deep in the earth and know our own earthy rootedness in the Mother Earth. Our eyes follow upwards the vertical line of its trunk and look upward to the stars, and are reminded of our spiritual heritage of sky and stars; we observe the life and beauty of its evergreen foliage and know our 'here and now-ness' to be the place where heaven and earth join.

We celebrate the rebirth of the eternal, immortal sun (the evergreen is a symbol of immortality), and are assured that this newly born light has returned to be among us once again, growing in strength and brilliance, bringing warmth and abundance, thereby renewing our lives.

Therefore, a modern Christmas or Yule tree, decorated with gingerbread cookies (warm, spicy, human/animal shapes), gilded apples (the fruit of immortality gilt with the gold of the sun) and lighted candles (warmth and light), tied with sprigs of mistletoe (the heavenly, magical All-Heal of the Druids) and topped with a shining star (the reborn sun, our deep, essential selves) is rich in the symbolism of our ancestors. Piled underneath with gifts for friends and family it becomes truly a shrine to the gods of light and warmth, prosperity and abundance, so sorely missed during the cold darkness of the winter.

The Native Americans celebrated this time of year as Earth Renewal Time, when Father Sun began his journey back from the North to warm Mother Earth and to bless her with new life. Prayer plumes for the year were made. Women ground cornmeal with a mortar and pestle and men mixed the kinnickinnick. Sweat lodge cleansings were done. Fires were put to sleep, then ritually relit. Thanks were given to the earth and sun for the gift of life.

This chapter would not be complete without a mention of Twelfth Night. Twelfth Night is a festival celebrated on the night of January 5th (Twelfth Night Eve). Twelfth Day is January 6th, twelve days after Christmas. In Christian terms the celebration marks the end of the twelve day Christmas season. January 6th was the feast of the Epiphany (which means 'manifestation'), when the birth of Jesus was made known to the world outside of his immediate family by the arrival of the 'Three Kings' or 'Magi.' Their gifts of gold (symbolic of his royalty), frankincense (symbolic of his high spiritual purpose) and myrrh (symbolic of the bitter suffering and death that lay ahead for him) acknowledged him, according to legend, as the King Foretold. And, indeed, by January 6th there is a noticeable difference in the length of the days—the Sun's rebirth has truly been made manifest to us all.

The "Twelves" were observed with much gaiety and celebration. It was a time of relaxation from the daily grind of work. Class distinctions, such as those between master and slave were temporarily suspended, as were most of the regular duties and regulations, and in general it was a time of freedom, merriment and good natured chaos.

Twelfth Night itself was celebrated as a night of great revelry and feasting, the highlight of which was the selection of the King who would rule over the night's revelries. (Sometimes the King was chosen at the beginning of the Twelves and ruled over the entire twelve days.) This monarch was referred to as King of the Bean or the Lord of Misrule. As the name suggests, the king was chosen by lot, the lot in this case being a bean baked into the Twelfth Night Cake. Sometimes a pea was also baked into the cake and the woman finding it became the Queen of the Bean (or Pea). That the king was chosen by lot, as well as the temporary suspension of the regulations of ordinary life, tips us off to the fact that the Mock King's true ancestry runs far back in time, to the Roman feast of Saturnalia, perhaps farther still.

Saturnalia was, for the Romans, the intercalary time between the ending of one year and the beginning of the next. It was celebrated over a several day period near the winter solstice. Like the Twelves, it was a time of merriment and chaos, during which the energies (both positive and negative) of the year just ending were allowed a time to be totally lived out to their fullest and craziest before being ritually ended and a new cycle begun. And indeed, running as an undercurrent to all the gaiety was the knowledge that the powers of darkness were at their strongest and that many unfriendly spirits were abroad. It was considered wise to be aware of this and take protective measures.

Saturnalia was a time when normal procedure was "stood on its head." Prisoners were freed and masters and slaves exchanged places. The Lord of Misrule reigning over all the festivities represented Saturn as both God of Abundance/Golden Age of Plenty and as Father Time/Grim Reaper. At the end of Saturnalia, the energy of the old having been completely lived out, the Lord of Misrule, Saturn's representative ended his own life to symbolize the end of one year (season, epoch, etc.) so that the new one could begin.

To put all this into a more current context, we can use the twelve days of Yuletide/Christmas as a time to really finish out the energies of the calendar year that is ending. The kids are all out of school on winter vacation and some of us are off work during much of this period of time. I find it to be a very relaxed, lazy time. There is very much of a "betwixt and between" energy happening. We might as well tune into it, use and enjoy it.

It is customary to make New Year's resolutions. This, of necessity, involves a certain amount of inner reflection on aspects of ourselves and our lives we would like to change. How about declaring the Twelves to be a "Time outside of Time," in which we allow ourselves time to relax, reflect, be with friends and have a good time while we consciously allow the old, no-longer-serving energies to depart, and contemplate the new seeds we would plant in the New Year to come? Revels and feasting (as described above) can be held on Twelfth Eve to mark the completion of this process.

ACTIVITIES

1) Artistically inclined parents can make up the above mentioned advent calendar, or one of the more traditional European ones can be purchased. Check local bookstores for these.

2) The lovely ceremony of creating a tabletop Advent garden has come to us from the Anthroposophical movement of Rudolf Steiner. It is about all the realms of nature preparing for the rebirth of light amid the darkness. Advent is calculated to begin four Sundays before

Christmas. In adapting this to Pagan usage, one can calculate it to begin four Sundays before the Solstice. Sunday is the appropriate day since it is the rebirth of the sun we are celebrating. Here are the steps for creating Advent gardens.

a) Use short, flexible, evergreen twigs and lay them out into a spiral on top of a cloth (white) covered table or sideboard. Set a white votive candle in the center of the spiral.

b) Collect and have in readiness:

— several small rocks, crystals and seashells
— small leaves, flowers, and apples
— feathers and/or small figurines of animals (favorite stuffed animals, if small enough, are great here)
— small human figures, whether they be tiny dolls or statues.

These are representative of the mineral realm, the plant realm, the animal realm and the human realm, respectively.

c) Also have ready four red or white candles, one for each week of Advent.

d) At night on the first Sunday of Advent, darken the room and let the first candle be lit and placed on the inside near the beginning of the spiral. The appropriate weekly verse is recited (see below). Then the children decoratively place their stones, crystals and seashells around the spiral of greenery.

e) On the remaining three Sundays of Advent the procedure is the same, with the plants, animal and human figurines used for the second, third and fourth weeks respectively.

Each candle is placed nearer to the center than the one before it. The center pillar candle should be lit on the Solstice, as part of the family celebration.

Here are the weekly verses:

i) The first light of Advent (light candle)
It is the light of stones.
Stones that live in crystals,
In seashells and in bones.

ii) The second light of Advent (light candle)
It is the light of plants.
Plants that reach up to the sun
And in the breeze dance.

iii) The third light of Advent (light candle)
It is the light of beasts.

The light of hope that we may see
The greatest in the least.

iv) The fourth light of Advent (light candle)
It is the light of Man.
The light of hope, the light of thought,
To give, and to understand.

3) An Advent wreath can be fashioned using evergreen branches twisted into a circle and tied together with floral wire. The wreath should be placed upon a table and four large red candles placed equidistant, creating a square within the circle. These candles are to be lit for each Sunday of Advent, until finally all four are burning together. We light them during dinnertime and/or storytime. If one can figure out a way to secure the candles in the wreath, the wreath can be suspended from a ceiling hook by four long red ribbons that have been wrapped around the wreath and the ends brought together in a knot above the wreath. Creating and using this wreath should, of course, be a family activity, with the jobs assigned in an age-appropriate manner.

4) Gift making and wrapping can actually begin in early or mid-November if need be (though it is sometimes hard for the children to keep secrets that long!). Parents should work with each child, helping to decide on makeable gift items for other members of the family. Knitting, crocheting, sewing, dollmaking, artwork, beadwork, baking—many crafts and skills can be a part of this.

5) Most of the above skills can also be used in ornament making. Each year we mix up a big batch of flour-salt-water dough and make ornaments, both for our tree and to give as gifts. Cookie cutters are very helpful here. We make trees, stars, bells, snow people, gingerbread people—anything seasonal that imagination can come up with. Solar symbols are particularly appropriate. We pierce a hole near the top for a ribbon to be placed and insert a toothpick in it. The ornaments are baked, painted, coated with shellac and allowed to dry thoroughly. They are then either placed upon the tree with special ceremony or wrapped to be given as gifts.

6) Since most of us do not live in rural areas where large fallen logs abound, the bringing in of the Yule log as done in the past is hardly possible. But we can create our own ceremonies around this, using as much of past lore as fits our needs. If it is possible to obtain a log eighteen inches or longer, a Yule log is still a possibility. The way we do it is to cut off enough of the underside of the log so that it has a flat bottom surface upon which to sit. This makes it secure enough

to put candles in without fear of them tipping over. Then we drill 13 holes in the top and place 13 thin red taper candles in them. We decorate the log with tendrils of ivy and sprigs of evergreen and holly tied on with red ribbons. We light the candles on Solstice night and allow them to burn all the way down. Alternatively, the log can be made without candles (though still decorated) and placed on the fire during the Solstice ritual. Part of the previous year's log should be used as kindling. And don't forget to sing that fine pagan carol "Deck the Halls" during your festivities!

7) Have a Twelfth Night party and wassail some fruit trees as part of it. Sit around your hearthfire (or a bonfire if weather permits) and pass around the wassail bowl, toasting the coming year/harvest.

RECIPES

SPECULAAS

4 cups sifted flour
1/2 teaspoon salt
4 teaspoons baking powder
1 tablespoon cinnamon
1 teaspoon nutmeg
1 teaspoon cloves
1/2 teaspoon white pepper
1/2 teaspoon powdered aniseed
1 cup softened butter
1 cup brown sugar
1 teaspoon grated lemon rind
1/2 cup slivered blanched almonds
1/3 to 1/2 cup milk

Sift together all of the dry ingredients. In another bowl cream sugar and butter until light and fluffy. Stir in the flour mixture and grated lemon rind. Add enough milk to make a soft dough. Roll out on a lightly floured board into a square about 1/2 inch thick. Cut into 3 inch squares (or use animal shaped cookie cutters). Place squares on greased baking sheet and sprinkle with almonds, pressing them in lightly. Bake in a preheated 350 degree oven for 15-20 minutes or until lightly browned. Makes about 40 cookies.

LUSSEKATTER

1/2 teaspoon dried saffron
3 tablespoons boiling water
2 tablespoons dry yeast
1 teaspoon salt
1/3 cup butter

1/4 cup sugar
1 cup scalded milk
1 egg
1/2 cup diced candied fruit rinds (can be omitted
    but increase amount of currants added)
1/2 cup currants
4 cups sifted flour
1/2 cup raisins
1 egg yolk

Soak the dried saffron in the boiling water for about 2 hours (you can omit this step by using powdered saffron). In a large warm bowl, dissolve the yeast in 1/4 cup warm water with 1 teaspoon sugar. Put remaining sugar, salt and butter into the scalded milk and stir until everything is melted. Strain the saffron and add the saffron water to the mixture.

Cool milk to lukewarm and pour it into the bowl. Beat the egg into it. Coat the currants and candied fruit rinds with 2 tablespoons flour. Gradually work the remaining flour into the yeast. Add fruits; turn out onto a floured board and knead for 10 minutes or until the dough is no longer sticky. Place the dough in a buttered bowl and roll it around to grease it well. Cover with a cloth and let it rise in a warm place until doubled in bulk (about 1 - 1 1/2 hours). Punch down and put onto the board and knead a few times. Divide the dough into 24 rounded buns. Punch 2 raisins into the buns to look like eyes and place on greased cookie sheet and let rise for 1/2 hour. Bake in a preheated 400 degree oven for 15 minutes. Lower the heat to 350 degrees and bake for another 20 minutes.

TWELFTH NIGHT CAKE

This is a dense, crumbly, old-world style fruitcake. Don't expect it to turn out like a packaged cake mix!

1 cup currants
1/2 cup raisins
1 cup dried prunes, chopped into large pieces
1 cup sultana raisins
1 cup chopped walnuts or pecans
2 cups flour
1 1/4 teaspoons nutmeg
1/4 teaspoon cinnamon
1/2 teaspoon soda
2 eggs, beaten
1/2 cup milk
1/2 cup honey
5/8 cup butter, melted
1 dried green pea
1 dried bean

Mix together fruit and nuts in a large bowl. Measure the spices and soda into a large measuring cup and add 1 cup of the flour; stir to mix in the spices. Pour this over the fruit, mixing well until the fruit is coated with flour. In a large bowl, beat the eggs lightly. Melt the butter and add the milk and honey and add this mixture to the eggs; stir together well. Add the fruit/flour mixture to the liquid ingredients and add the final cup of flour; stir until blended. Place in a greased and floured 9 or 10 inch round cake pan and carefully insert pea and bean within the batter. Bake at 325 degrees for 1 1/4 hours or till done.

Note: It is wise to use a bean whose color will contrast with the other ingredients to prevent the possibility of broken teeth or choking on the part of enthusiastic cake eaters. It is also wise, if sharing this cake with very small children, to note in some manner where the bean and pea are placed by marking the spot so choice may be exercised in giving them these particular pieces.

WASSAIL BOWL

This is a close relative and variation on Lamb's Wool.

18 crab apples (regular ones will do)
2 1/2 cups brown sugar
3 quarts ale
1 bottle sweet sherry
5 slices fresh ginger root or 1 teaspoon powdered ginger
1/2 teaspoon powdered cloves
6 eggs, separated
1 cup cognac, heated
10 slices buttered toast, cut in quarters

Sprinkle the apples with 1/2 cup brown sugar and bake in a preheated 350 degree oven for about 30 minutes. In a large saucepan heat ale, sherry and spices. Beat egg yolks until thick. Beat egg whites until very stiff and fold thoroughly into the yolks. Pour the ale mixture into the eggs in a thin stream, beating hard. Put the hot apples in a heated bowl, add egg-ale mixture and cognac. Pass toast to dip or float in mugs. Makes 18 drinks.

As with the Lamb's Wool recipe for Samhain this can be made in a nonalcoholic manner. Use apple cider instead of ale and omit the sherry and cognac.

FAMILY YULE RITUAL

On the night of the winter solstice, Yule can be celebrated with this family ritual.

Needed: Yule log with holes drilled in it to hold enough red candles for everyone, pine incense, big red or white candle.

PRIESTESS:
> For a few months the days have been growing shorter,
> And the nights longer.
> After today, little by little,
> The hours of light will increase.

The days will grow longer
Until once again it is Summer.

PRIEST:

We celebrate now the time of midwinter
Which is called Yule.
It marks the birth of the Sun.
Let us call on the Magic Spirits
To speak of this time.

As the quarters are invoked, the quarter candles are lit.

EAST:

Winter is the time:
For cold winds and freezing breezes.
Spirits of the air, be with us tonight.

SOUTH:

Winter is the time:
For sitting in front of roaring fires for warmth,
And blazing candles for light.
Spirits of the fire, be with us tonight.

WEST:

Winter is the time:
Of rain falling, water turning to ice,
And Jack Frost nipping at us.
Spirits of the water, be with us tonight.

NORTH:

Winter is the time:
When the earth is bare,
Most trees have no leaves,
No food is growing now.
Spirits of the earth, be with us now.

PRIESTESS:

Goddess of all seasons, we see you now
As mother with child.
Be with us tonight.

PRIEST:

God of all seasons, we see you now
As the dying sun, and yet also
As a tiny baby, the sun reborn.
Be with us tonight.

PRIESTESS:

> As the darkness increases,
> We feel the death of the Sun-God approaching.
> But in the darkest of winter,
> He is reborn as the light of the infant sun.
> It is the Great Mother who gives birth to him,
> Who brings the Child of Promise to Earth.
> It is the Lord of Light and Life who is born again!

Priestess lights the big red or white candle.

> The year wheel turns
> And light returns!

All join hands and circle around the altar chanting.

ALL:

> The sun, the light, shining bright
> Returns, returns, returns, returns (three times, or more as desired)
>
> Arthur, Osiris, Apollo,
> Helios, Lugh, Mithra, Mabon (three times)

As the last phrase fades away all take their places in the circle. Candles are passed out to each person.

PRIEST:

> Now, starting with the youngest, we will each light our candles from the big Yule Candle, and make a silent wish for the new year. Then we will set our candles into the holes in the Yule log, and return to our places in the circle.

If a Yule log is an impossibility this can be done with votive candles and they can be set on the hearth or the altar when lit. When all have finished with their candles, the quarters are dismissed and the quarter candles are blown out.

EAST:

> Spirits of Air, we thank you for being with us tonight
> And now bid you farewell.

SOUTH:

> Spirits of Fire, we thank you for being with us tonight
> And now bid you farewell.

WEST:

> Spirits of Water, we thank you for being with us tonight
> And now bid you farewell.

NORTH:

> Spirits of Earth, we thank you for being with us tonight
> And now bid you farewell.

PRIESTESS:

> Lovely Mother, Tiny Child, we thank you for blessing us with your presence tonight, and as the days grow longer we will know you are always with us.
>
> This rite is ended. Merry meet and merry part!

ALL:

> And Merry meet again!

The candles in the Yule log or on the hearth should be allowed to burn until gone, or as long as possible.

MUSIC

Many of the current Christmas carols have pagan origins. Several can be rewritten or restored. Some, such as "Deck the Halls," are fine just the way they are. Below is a rewrite of "The Holly and The Ivy" that I did for last Yule.

THE HOLLY AND THE IVY

Margie McArthur   traditional

1. The__ hol-ly and the   i - vy   when they are both full   grown; Of__
Cho. O the ris-ing of   the   sun___ and the run-ning of the   deer The_

all the trees that are   in the wood The__   hol - ly bears the__ crown.
play-ing of   the___   pipes and drums, Sweet_ sing-ing round the__ fire.

2.   The Holly King has ruled us, All through the waning days.
     As chosen of the Summer Maid Through the autumn's chill he stays.

3.   But the Holly King must fall As is the ancient way.
     And the Reborn Sun the Oaken King, In turn shall have his day.

4.   As wren gives way to robin And fall to winter tide;
     The dying sun to newborn sun, And the darkness turns to light.

5.   The holly bears a prickle, As sharp as any thorn.
     And the Mother bore the Holy Child On Solstice Day in the morn.

6.   The Holly and the Ivy. Now both are full well grown.
     But the Holly King to the Oaken King Must now give up the crown.

7.   But as the year wheel turneth, The Oak King has his sway,
     Soon the battle's fought and the Holly King, Again will have his way.

THE THIRTEEN DAYS OF YULETIDE
by Marian Geraghty and Morgyn Owens-Celli

On the first day of Yuletide my true love gave to me
A Golden Bough in an oak tree.

On the second day...two lovers loving...
On the third day...three pentagrams...
On the fourth day...four blowing winds...
On the fifth day...five trees of earth...
On the sixth day...six ways of sensing...
On the seventh day...seven cauldrons swirling...
On the eighth day...eight Sabbat fires...
On the ninth day...nine stones for stepping...
On the tenth day...ten pagans dancing...
On the eleventh day...eleven stags a leaping...
On the twelfth day...twelves signs of turning...
On the thirteenth day...thirteen moons a shining...

Apple Orchard Wassail #1 (Poem)

Here's to thee, old apple tree,
Whence thou may'st bud and whence thou may'st blow,
And whence thou may'st bear apples enow.
Hats full, caps full, bushel, bushel sacks full,
And my pockets full too! Hurrah!

Apple Orchard Wassail#2 (Poem)

Stand fast root, bear well top,
Pray God send us a good howling crop.
Every twig, apples big, Every bough, apples enow.
Hats full, caps full, full quarter sacks full,
Holla, boys, holla!
Huzza!

WINTER KING

words, music and
arrangement
© 1992 Phillip Wayne

1. Win-ter_ King, your_ hand is cold, up_ - on the earth, the_ snow, A
2. Win-ter_ King, I_ see your hand in_ soft car-ess on_ earth, Pre -

fea-ther_ blan-ket_ soft and old is_ marked by stag and_ doe
pares her-self for_ com-ing spring, and_ for the year's re_ - birth

Cho. Win-ter_ King, I feel your breath, like ice up-on the air, It

brings in life by bring-ing death to heath and hound and_ hare

3. Winter King, your eyes are bright, They twinkle in the sun
   That sees the day, and flees the night When winter's course is run.

4. Winter King, your voice a-wail Is heard throughout the land
   In every house, in every home Where burns a yule-log brand.

5. Winter King, this is your time, The ancient time of Yule.
   When snow is covered by jewel-rime, And winter plays the fool.

THE WOOD CUTTER'S SONG

Traditional arr. J. Paul Espinoza
further arr. ©1993 Phillip Wayne

Logs to burn, Logs to burn, Logs to save the coal a turn

Here's a word__ to make you wise when you hear_ the woodsman's cries

1. Oak - en logs willl warm you well that are old and dry
2. Birch____ logs will burn too fast chest-nut scarce at all

Logs of pine will sweet__ - ly smell but the sparks will fly
Haw - thorn logs are good__ to last Cut them in the fall

3. Holly logs will burn like wax, You may burn them green;
   Elm logs like to smoldering flax, No flame to be seen.

4. Beech logs for winter time, Yew logs as well;
   Green Elder logs it is a crime For any man to sell.

5. Pear logs and apple logs They will scent your room;
   Cherry logs across the dogs Smell like flower of broom.

6. Ash logs smooth and gray, Burn them green or old
   Buy up all that come your way Worth their weight in gold.

WINTER'S CHILDREN

1. Come, my friend and quick-ly we'll go, a - fol - low - ing the
2. Watch the flames as they dance higher a fu - ner - ar - ry

win - ter - y roe - buck Up the moun - tain thick with soft snow to
old year's pyre to dance the new year in with fire where

where they build the Yule fire. Sleep moth-er earth your child is a -
moun - tain meets the gray sky.

born - ing sleep till the land in the Spring has it's morn - ing

bless win - ter's child - ren and sleep.

3. Come and watch, the old year dies, As all things must we cannot deny,
    And like us all returns by and by, To sip life from a god's horn.

4. Dance until the new year is born, Whirling, twirling up 'til the morn,
    Calling to the unicorn And dancing in the cold snow.

5. Like a babe in her mother's arms, Days grow longer upon the earth,
    Warming, sounding spring's first alarms See the year giving birth.

Twelfth Night, or King and Queene (Poem)
by Robert Herrick

Now, now the mirth comes
With the cake full of plums,
Where Beane's the King of the sport here;
Beside we must know,
The Pea also
Must revell, as Queene, in the Court here.

Begin then to chuse,
(This night as ye use)
Who shall for the present delight here,
Be a King by the lot,
And who shall not
Be Twelfth-day Queene for the Night here.

Which knowne, let us make
Joy-sops with the cake;
And let not a man then be seen here,
Who unurg'd will not drinke
To the base to the brinke
A health to the King and the Queene here.

Next crowne the bowle full
With gentle lambs-wooll;
Add sugar, nutmeg and ginger,
With stores of ale too;
And thus ye must doe
To make the wassaile a swinger.

Give then to the King
And Queene wassailing;
And though with ale ye be whet here;
Yet part ye from hence,
As free from offence,
As when ye innocent met here.

RIME

words and music
©1986 Phillip Wayne

1. Rime, rime, cover the ground like a cold, cold glove made of elven frost Win-ter
2. Snow, snow soft as a fair-y song White, white milk of the un-i-corn Down, down,

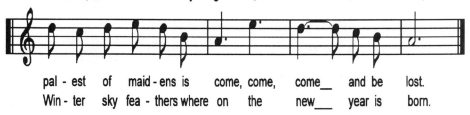

pal - est of maid - ens is come, come, come__ and be lost.
Win - ter sky fea - thers where on the new__ year is born.

3. Like a babe in her mother's arms Days grow longer upon the earth
   Warming, Sounding spring's first alarms See the year giving birth

And finally, here is the poem for Lucia Day.

Lucia

The night of the year is upon us,
Winter enfolds us in icy arms.
The summer sun is dying, dying,
The night is long and we are afraid.

But through the darkness comes a light,
Shining dimly, shining bright.
Lucia comes and brings her light,
Brings to her people much delight.

Lucia Queen comes to us with song.
The winter doesn't seem as long.
She sings of sun's returning
She sings of year wheel's turning.

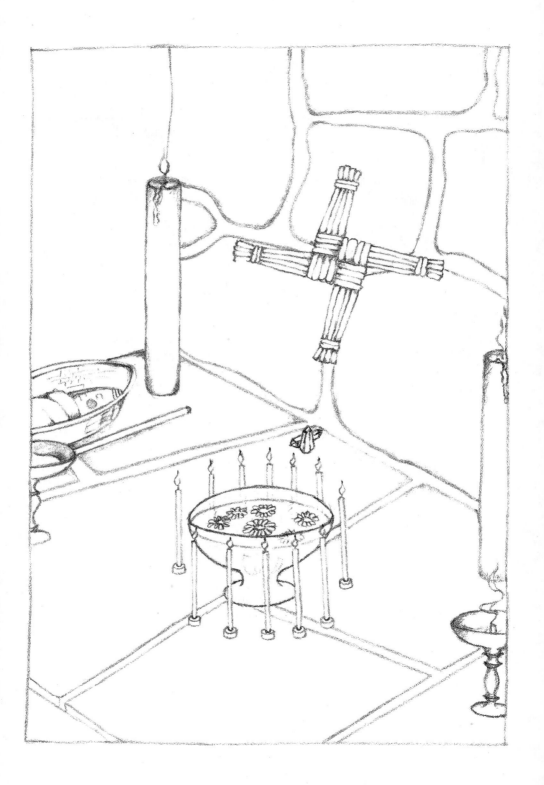

CHAPTER 7
IMBOLC
February 2nd

Return to us, O Thou White Swan,
Bride of the Golden Hair
Ed Fitch

Imbolc is another one of those favorite times for our children. It is also called Brigid or Brigantia, after the Celtic Goddess Brigid, and it is sometimes called Candlemas, after a Christian celebration occurring at this time of year. The Christian Church instituted the feasts of Candlemas, St. Blaise and St. Brigid in early February because it was a time when, especially in the Celtic countries, people were used to celebrating a fire festival. Candlemas is a feast where candles are blessed for the liturgical year; St. Blaise is a feast where throats are blessed using two candles crossed together in an X shape. The Celtic feast of Brigid fell on the first day of February.

Brigid was unarguably one of the most important and most beloved of the Celtic Goddesses. Although seen more as a virgin (in the old sense of the word) or sister goddess than a mother goddess, she is definitely connected with fertility, as well as with the healing, smithcrafting, all cultural arts, and the fires of inspiration that burn behind all these. In Ireland and parts of Scotland she is still commemorated to this day.

In her Christianized form of St. Brigid, she took on many of the aspects of the Goddess Brigid, as well as being regarded as the foster mother of the child Jesus. In Celtic lands, the foster mother frequently was at least as important and influential as the birth mother of a young boy since it was part of the culture to "foster out" children. What this is really saying is that the new religion was nourished in its growth by the previous one.

Since Brigid was, at this time of year, seen as a maiden goddess who (in some of the Scottish stories) is rescued from the Cailleach (Hag) of Winter by her lover, Angus, I've always found it interesting that St. Valentine's Day, with its emphasis on love, falls two weeks later, on February 14th. Could it be that February 14th is really the feast of Angus?

The Romans celebrated Lupercalia, a feast of purification and fertility, near this time.

Imbolc is a time of purifications, of renewal, of initiations, and of fire in its light-giving aspect, rather than its heat-giving aspect. Candles are made to recognize this aspect and in observance of Imbolc's theme of purification, pre-spring cleaning is sometimes begun now. In keeping with the theme of renewal and initiations, this is a good time to make formal promises and dedications to the idea of following the Craft of the Wise as a life path.

To celebrate this day we make Bride's Crosses and candles, and the children perform the Imbolc play. We read aloud stories of Brigid, the Cailleach, and Angus the Ever Young, and we ceremonially light the Brigid candle.

The candlemaking project is the biggest part of our Imbolc festival. We devote the better part of a day to this celebration. The candle making itself can take several hours depending on how many people are participating. We end things up with a potluck dinner, followed by a ritual in the early evening.

ACTIVITIES

CANDLEMAKING

For the wax, beeswax is by far the best, wonderfully alive and sweet swelling, but hard to locate inexpensively unless you have nearby beekeepers. Paraffin will do if you cannot get beeswax. Going to get the wax is part of the magic for me. The beekeeper who supplies us lives in the countryside nearby and the drive to his house is quite a beautiful one.

If you use paraffin, you will need to find some stearin. Stearin is a necessary addition to the making of candles with paraffin as it helps to dissolve the dye, harden the wax and make the candle burn longer. Hobby shops will probably have it, along with some instructions for how much of it to use.

It is also a good idea to locate some colored thin strips of beeswax for use in decorating the candles after they are finished. Sources for finding some of these things will be listed at the back of the book in the Resources section.

You will also need candlewicking. This can usually be found in hardware stores or hobby shops. Obtain also something to be used as weights on the ends of the wicking. These keep the wick straight by their weight while you are dipping. We use small metal washers (shaped like rings) about 1/2 to 3/4 inches across. If you do not want to dip candles you can make molded candles instead. Many things can be used for molds: old margarine or yogurt tubs, empty cans—just about anything that has a large enough opening to slide the hardened candle out. You can also fill an old dishpan with damp sand, dig interestingly shaped holes in it and pour the wax into it. To get the wicking to stay where you want it in molded candles, you need to attach a weight to the bottom and tie a pencil or stick to the top, setting it sideways across the top of the mold (see illustration).

A wax thermometer would be a handy thing to have as the wax needs to be about 180 degrees F before it is ready to be poured into the molds. If you can arrange to set your filled mold in a container of water so that the level of the water is the same as the level of the wax, the candle will harden faster and the finish of the candle will be enhanced. After the candle has started to set, poke a hole down the center near the wick with a stick or ice pick and pour a little more wax into this area. Since the candle shrinks as it cools, this will help to keep the top level, and may need to be done more than once.

Let the candle cool completely before removing it from the mold. If it does not seem to want to come out of the mold, set it in the refrigerator for 30–40 minutes, and try again. The chill of being in the refrigerator should contract the wax enough to enable the candle to slide easily out of the mold.

We usually make dipped candles. We set up our area right after breakfast is done. Newspapers are laid out all over the dining room floor and on the dining room table. The camping stove is brought in from its usual home in the garage and installed at one end of the table. A large, deep pot, no more than half full of water and covered, is put to boil on the campstove. Another pot, of a size that will fit loosely (but not tip over) into the first pot, is filled with wax to within about two to three inches of the brim. It is then set within the first pot. As the water boils in the first pot, the wax in the second pot will begin to melt. The melting can take a long time with a block of wax large enough to make dipped candles, so it is best to schedule some activity during this time, such as lunch preparation or ritual rehearsal.

The wicks can be prepared during this time. Measure a piece of wicking as long as you want your candle plus about four or five inches more and cut it. At one end tie the weight. It is now ready for use.

Put a pot of cool water near the pot of melted wax. This is for dipping the candle in to help it harden faster.

When the wax has fully melted, wicks with weights on them are handed out and everyone forms a line. One by one people come up to the campstove and carefully dip their wick into the pot of wax for no longer than two or three seconds (longer than that will remelt the wax, causing it to run off the wick), keeping it as straight as possible. We put a chair by the stove for the

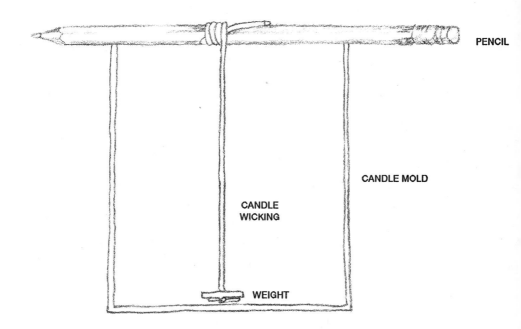

little ones to stand on so they can reach the pot of wax more easily, and a grownup is always standing by to help those who need it. When the wick has been dipped into first the wax and then the cool water, the person moves on and the next person in line moves up and dips their wick into the wax, and so on.

The whole process is long and can get boring to some, so we usually have a person reading to us from a book of Celtic legends and stories of Brigid. Our favorite is the one from *Celtic Wonder Tales* by Ella Young. It is also wise to have some song ideas ready. When hunger hits we take a lunch break, eating the snacky kinds of things we prepared earlier.

When people have made as many candles as they care to, we bring out the package of colored strips of wax, and knives for cutting it, and people can decorate their candles as they wish, cutting the colored wax into long, thin strips and creating a candy cane effect or a spiraled design (both much beloved of some of the small ones in our household). Cutting short, thin strips and creating a starlike pattern is also nice. Obviously the age of the child will determine the degree of sophistication of the design. Remember, the process is often more important than the end result. We actually leave many of our candles undecorated, preferring them that way.

MAKING BRIDE'S BED

Another custom associated with Imbolc, the Feast of Brigid, is that of making a Brigid's Bed. This is done to welcome Her back—to welcome the return of spring from the land of winter. By the way, Bride is pronounced 'Breed.'

To do this begin by cleaning your hearth thoroughly and laying a fire in it (do the cleaning early in the day). Do not kindle the fire yet. Then make a "bed" for Brigid by arranging a pillow and blanket near the hearth; it can be whatever size is convenient. The bed can be simple or fancy, whatever you feel like doing (it can even be made up in a small basket). If you do not have a fireplace and hearth then arrange the bed near your kitchen stove. In the evening, using one of the candles you made earlier that day, ritually invite Brigit into your home by lighting the candle and using it to light your hearth fire, while reciting a poem or incantation to her, either your own or one of the following:

1. Three ladies came from the east,
   With gold, with silver, with iron wrought fair.
   Return to us, O Thou White Swan,
   Bride of the Golden Hair.
   (old English charm, adapted by Ed Fitch)

2. Brigit, excellent woman, sudden flame,
   May the bright fiery sun take us
   To the lasting kingdom.

3. Bride is come, Bride is welcome!
   Bride is come, Bride is welcome!
   Bride is come, Bride is welcome!

In one variation of this custom, a phallic wand or club was placed beside the bed as it lay near the hearth. If the ashes in the hearth were found to be disturbed in the morning this was regarded as a sign the year ahead would be prosperous. The God had come in the night to impregnate the Goddess; bounty was assured.

THE LIGHTING OF THE BRIGID CANDLE

At Brigid's shrine in Cill Dara (Kildare), Ireland, a perpetual fire burned. No one knows when this custom started but it predated the Christian era by many years. The fire was tended by nineteen priestesses (a role later taken over by the nuns of St. Brigid). According to legend, on the twentieth night the fire was tended by Brigid herself. Narrow-minded thinkers extinguished this flame in 1220 A.D. but public outcry was so great that the flame was relit by local church authorities. It was permanently extinguished during the Reformation.

Thinking about all this caused me to want to relight Brigid's Fire, the fire of inspiration, healing and fertility. The world is sorely in need of Her radiance and blessing, so I created this mini-ritual, which can be performed on its own, or as part of another ritual.

For this ceremony all the women present gather around a large (6–8 inch) pillar candle of a color reminiscent of fire (sometimes these pillar candles can be found with three wicks). Joining hands, all breathe quietly together and link energies. When this has been done, they together recite the following:

> As once Your eternal flame burned
> Both day and night in Your shrine,
> So do we light this candle to You, Blessed Brigid,
> Bringer of light and fertility.
>
> May the light of Your inspiration shine upon us.
> May You inspire us in our arts, our music, our crafts.
> May You guide us as we heal.
> Blessed One, Fair One, this do we ask of You,
> As we offer to You
> The inextinguishable light of our love and homage.

BRIGID'S CROSS

An old custom that is part celebrating the feast of St. Brigid in Ireland even today is the making of Brigid's Crosses. These crosses are equal armed crosses, woven of rushes or straw.

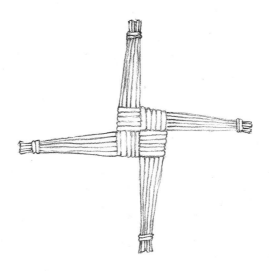

RECIPES

In Ireland it was customary around the time of Imbolc to gather seaweed for use as fertilizer. Many of these vegetables from the sea were routinely used as a part of the diet, due to their availability, good taste and nutritional value.

This recipe uses porphyra (known as laver in Britain, sloke in Ireland), sold in the United States under its Japanese name of nori.

LAVERBREAD

4 sheets of nori cut into 1 inch squares OR
   1/2 to 1 ounce laver, toasted, cut into small pieces
1 cup oat flour (grind in a blender) OR
   1 cup whole wheat pastry flour
1 cup rolled oats
1/4 teaspoon salt
1/4 cup oil
1/2 cup hot water

Stir the dry ingredients together in a large bowl. Add the nori and stir. Mix the liquid ingredients together in a measuring cup and pour into dry ingredients. Stir until it acquires a doughlike consistency, adding more flour if needed. Roll out on a flour covered board to 1/2 inch thick. Cut into circles (or other shapes) with a drinking glass or cookie cutter. Bake in a preheated 400 degree oven for 20 minutes. Or flatten them out and fry on a griddle as you would a pancake, until done. An alternative method is to cook the nori in a small amount of water until it is thick and pasty. Add this to the bowl and increase the amount of flour until the correct consistency is achieved.

BRIDECAKES

1/2 cup butter
1/4 cup honey
2 cups oat flour or wheat flour
1/4 teaspoon salt
1/2 teaspoon baking soda
1 cup rolled oats
1/2 cup currants
1/4 cup buttermilk

Cream butter and honey together. Mix the dry ingredients together and add the currants, stirring to coat them with flour. Stir dry ingredients into the butter-honey mixtures and add enough buttermilk to make a dough. Roll into balls and flatten onto a greased cookie sheet. With a knife mark each of them with a Bride's Cross (+). Bake in a preheated 350 degree oven for 15 minutes.
Serve with a glass of fresh buttermilk.

FAMILY IMBOLC RITUAL

This ritual is a play, to be performed by your children and their friends. The narrator can be an adult or one of the children who reads well. Thanks, once again, to JoAnn Adams for this one.

Cast of characters: Mother, father, their children, Spring Maiden, Young King.

Necessary props: gold crown, sword and cape, wreath of flowers and veil, loaf of fresh bread, chalice of water, dish of salt, incense, candelabrum, lots of candles, a new fire laid in the hearth, chimes.

Scene 1

Children are asleep on the floor. Father enters from offstage.

FATHER:

Children, children, it's time to get up! Hurry! Today is the feast of candles and we have a lot of work to do. We must get ready for the Spring Maiden and the Young King.

Children wake up. Mother enters.

MOTHER:

Yes, there is a lot to do. (To Father:) You must scrub the hearth and lay a fresh fire. And I must bake a new loaf of bread. (To a child:) You must polish the candlesticks and fetch fresh candles from the pantry. (To another child:) You must sweep the floor and lay down new rushes and sprinkle fresh herbs. And we must all clean the house today from top to bottom in honor of the Spring Maiden and the Young King.

Everyone scurries around sweeping, cleaning, dusting.

NARRATOR:

And so, because the father was a good father and loved his family and helped to keep things well ordered, he scrubbed the hearth until it was bright and new and laid a fresh, unlit fire in it. And because the mother was a good mother and loved her family and helped to keep things well ordered, she measured and sifted and kneaded the dough until she had a new loaf of bread with lots of good things in it. And because the children were good children, and loved their family and helped to keep things well ordered, they helped with the sweeping and dusting, the picking up and the putting away. They all cleaned the attic, the living room, the root cellar, the goat shed, the chicken coop, the bedrooms, the playroom and

the woodshed. They cleaned under things, on things, behind things.
Why they even cleaned in places that no one ever saw! They even
cleaned up the old cobwebs so the spiders could spin shiny new
webs in honor of the Spring Maiden and the Young King. And when
they were done, they set the table with the new bread and cider,
with fresh candles and flowers and with a goblet of water, a pinch of
salt and some incense to sweeten the air.

Scene 2

*Table with above mentioned items. Loaf should already be sliced and there
should be enough bread and cider to feed everyone who is present, including
the audience. Cast enters and Father lights the candles. Mother puts salt in the
water and stirs, then carries goblet around the room and touches everyone with
it.*

MOTHER:
> With water and earth I bless this house
> And all who are within;
> That we may be made clean and pure
> To greet the Spring Maiden and the Young King.

*Father lights incense and carries it around the room, censing everyone as he
goes.*

FATHER:
> With fire and air I bless this house
> And all who are within;
> That we may be made clean and pure
> To greet the Spring Maiden and the Young King.

NARRATOR:
> And then they all sat down and waited.

*There is a knocking from without. Mother goes to the door and shows the two
guests to the table and seats them in the best seats.*

FATHER:
> We are honored to welcome you to our home.

MOTHER:
> We invite you to share this feast with us as we mark this time of
> cleansing and beginning anew. And in token of this do I light these
> new candles for the first time.

Mother and father serve bread and juice to all.

NARRATOR:

And what a feast they had! For they had invited all their friends and neighbors and there was singing and dancing long into the night. And just as the clock struck midnight the Young King and the Spring Maiden stood up and spoke.

YOUNG KING:

My friends, we are honored by the love you have shown us here today. Never has there been such a fine feast. Nor such merry singing and dancing. But now we must take our leave of you and continue our journey. For we have far to go and much to accomplish before we meet with you again.

SPRING MAIDEN:

But before we go, in token of the love that is shared between the races of mortal beings and the ancient ones, I renew the gift of fire, the gift of life. (Takes a candle from the table and lights the fire in the fireplace.) May your home always be a beacon of light and truth.

YOUNG KING:

May the creatures of the wild places, forest and fen, willingly share of their bounty in answer to your need.

SPRING MAIDEN:

May your fields and cattle be fruitful. May your granaries be full and may your hearts be overflowing with love for each other.

SPRING MAIDEN & YOUNG KING:

Thus do we bless you, each and everyone!

MUSIC

SOUL WALKER

words and music
Phillip Wayne

1. Ga - ther round the fire my child - ren, And I'll sing of long a - go,
2. Snowflakes are her fro - zen tears, and Cold the breath the harsh winds blow.

When a pearl white faer - y maid - en Left her foot - prints in the snow.
Faer - y hills are glisten-ing soft - ly, Glistening, glistening in the snow.

Walk - er in the si - lent plac - es, Walk - er where no man must go.

Our a - lone - ness cries out to you, Walk - er in the snow.

3. Shed no tears we are her children, Winter passes, this I know.
   Snowfall glistening, we are listening For her footfall in the snow.

4. Laughing round the needfire dancing, Round and round and round we go.
   Love our Lady sends her children, Dancing in the glistening snow.

AN FAOILLEACH

(pronounced "AnFULikh", means "Wolf Month")

words and music
Phillip Wayne

1. Brith - id came stri - ding through ice and through snow, Ice-bound the
2. Dag - da, her birth - ing, is fled from Aes Sidhe, and An - gus is

steel__ that swings by her side. Si - lent, be - hind her the
fled from the Faoill-each's wild cry. The fort - ress is emp-ty that

wolf walk-ing slow, Guard-ing her foot-steps as on - ward to
stands by the sea, As emp-ty as e - ver the not - world might

go, Where none but the strong-est may ride. An faoill - each, an
be, Were ne - ver a god-ling to die.

faoill-each, I heard the wind wail, An faoill-each, an faoill-each, and

tell of her need. An faoill-each, an faoill-each, the cry told a

tale, An faoill - each, and faoill - each, of Brithid. (The)

3. A wolf pup will love her, a wolf pup alone.
    The wolfling has bound her until she is free.
    She walked on the white moors when winter was grown,
    A cry for the Dagda and seeking her own
    A bringing the wolf month to thee.

CHAPTER 8

OSTARA

Spring Equinox - March 21st

Spring, O Spring! What did you bring?
I have brought you three gifts:
The first gift — cattle in the field,
The second gift — plowing in the field,
The third gift — the flutter of the bees.
And one gift more — happy be the world.
old Russian spring song

Easter, Eostre and Ostara are all names used to refer to the Spring or Vernal Equinox. Eostre was a Teutonic fertility goddess and her name is probably a variant of Ishtar or Astarte. The Christian feast of Easter, which falls anywhere from right after the Spring Equinox to right before Beltane, celebrates roughly the same ideas as our Pagan Eostre: the sun/son rises, conquers death/winter and makes possible new life for all/food will now be able to be grown. You get the idea.

Once again it is a time for Ecumenism. Many of the symbols used by Christians at Easter time are quite appropriately used by Pagans at Equinox. And why not, since they were ours to start with! Or maybe it is more accurate to say that some of them are universal symbols of springtime and the new tide of life that is flowing through the earth. So we can happily await the Eostre bunny, knowing that the hare was one of the sacred beasts of the Goddess as well as a symbol of fertility which is very appropriate at this time of year. And we can dye our eggs (magical amulets of fertility and prosperity and protection) beautiful hues and hide them for the children to find, secure in the knowledge that this little observance is truly a ritual celebrating springtime and the new life that is to be found all around us.

Our family has a few tried and true customs at this time of year. We take the somewhat ecumenical approach mentioned above. Our springtime celebration extends between the Spring Equinox and Easter Sunday. We schedule our events within that time frame as seems appropriate to what is happening outside in the earth's cycle.

We read stories about Demeter and Persephone, and other stories related to springtime. We eat Hot Cross Buns on Good Friday. Rounded buns with a central disc like a wheel were found in the volcanic ruins at Herculaneum. Hot cross buns bear an even-armed cross on them, symbolic of the fire of the sun, which has returned with the lengthening of days, and also the four seasons of the year, the four directions, and all those other meaningful fours.

We dye and decorate eggs using natural dyes. A chart detailing this procedure will be found below. Some eggs are blown, a thread put through them and they are hung on our Eostre tree. Some are hard boiled before dying then saved for the egg hunt. Sometimes we try to decorate our eggs in the old Ukranian style referred to as Pysanki. This is a batik-type technique using beeswax and a special tool (called a kitska) to paint intricate designs on eggshells, which are then dyed. By planning it out ahead, having a knowledge of what one color will look like on top of another color, and scraping off part of the wax between coats of dye, incredibly beautiful eggs can be produced.

The Eostre bunny comes to our house and brings beautiful baskets, though we usually save this particular custom for Easter Sunday, so the children are not too far out of step with their friends. Also we plant some seeds, usually as part of our Ostara ritual. The seeds can be sprouted in little pots, carefully tended, and then planted outside in the garden when the weather permits. Sometimes we line a small wicker basket with foil, fill it with earth and plant wheat berries in it. They sprout and within a few weeks we have a wheatgrass nest to lay our Eostre eggs in.

Springtime is also a time for cleaning. The cleaning and purification that was begun at Imbolc can be completed now and a ritual devised around this. Cleaning is in itself a ritual—one of clearing away what is no longer needed in order to make room for growth, change and newness.

ACTIVITIES

THE EOSTRE TREE

The Eostre tree deserves a little more mention. To make one, you need a rather large branch with lots of little branchlets on it. If you cannot find one, perhaps a suitable tree will give you its permission to take a branch. Don't forget to express your appreciation.

Plant this into a pot of soil or sand, anchoring it firmly. Try to find a branch that is just beginning to show young green leaves, or perhaps look for a pussy willow. In some areas, the making of an Eostre tree is best left until Easter rather than the equinox due to the growing season. A few more weeks can make a difference in the availability of leafing branches. Carefully blow some eggs and decorate them. Tie a short piece of string, ribbon or yarn to a short match and carefully insert it into the hole at the top of the egg. Then tie the other end to one of the branches of the Eostre tree.

BLOWING EGGS

The procedure for blowing eggs is as follows: Use a pin and make two holes, one at each end of the egg, opposite each other. Begin blowing, slowly and steadily (it takes a while) until the egg seeps out. This can be saved for use in cooking. Rinse the empty egg shell under cool water and allow to dry. It is now ready for use.

DYEING EGGS WITH NATURAL DYES

To dye eggs with natural dyes is always a real experience. The colors are very subtle, and the children are always amazed that a handful of onion skins or red cabbage produce the colors that they do. Boil a large handful or two of the dye material in two or three cups of water for about ten minutes. Watch it to make sure the pot does not boil dry! Strain, pour into cups, add one tablespoon vinegar to fix the dye, and let it sit for a few minutes, then it is ready to dye the eggs.

Colors and materials to produce them:

Deep golden to light golden brown—skins from brown onions
Light blue—red cabbage leaves
Light blue-grey to dark grey-violet—blueberries
Yellow—turmeric or saffron powder
Pink—beet juice
Pale orange—carrot juice
Light purple—grape juice

It is not necessary to boil the juices; just add the vinegar. If you tie a tiny leaf or branch carefully to the egg before dyeing, it's pattern should remain on the egg.

RECIPES

HOT CROSS BUNS

2 tablespoons dry yeast
2 tablespoons sugar
1/2 cup lukewarm milk
1 cup milk
3 1/2 - 4 1/2 cups flour
1/2 teaspoon salt
1 teaspoon allspice
1 teaspoon cinnamon
2 eggs
4 tablespoons unsalted, softened butter
2/3 cup sultanas or other raisins (or currants)
1 lightly beaten egg white

Sprinkle yeast and sugar into lukewarm milk and let stand for a few minutes. Stir to dissolve yeast.

Sift together dry ingredients into a large bowl. Make a well in the center and pour in the yeasty milk. Drop in eggs and beat all very well until flour is absorbed. Cut the butter into small bits and beat it in. Add up to 1 cup more flour, 1 tablespoon at a time until dough is soft enough to be gathered up into a ball. Work with fingers and knead lightly until dough is smooth and elastic. Shape into a ball and set in a greased bowl to rise for 45 minutes. Transfer dough to a breadboard and punch down, then knead in the raisins.

For each bun pull off a piece of dough and roll into a ball about 1 1/2 inches in diameter. Place on a greased baking sheet. Save a hunk of dough and roll it with your hands into small thin strips. These can be cut and put onto the buns forming a cross shape. Let the buns rise for 15-20 minutes, then brush on the beaten egg white to create a glaze and bake in a preheated 450 degree oven for 15 minutes.

EOSTRE BREAD

This beautifully shaped bread has served as a centerpiece on our Eostre table many times.

1 cup milk
1/2 cup sweet butter
4 eggs
2 tablespoons yeast
1/2 cup warm water
1 tablespoon honey
1 1/2 teaspoons salt
1 teaspoon anise seed, crushed
2 tablespoons dried grated orange or lemon peel
1/3 cup honey
6–6 1/2 cups flour (whole wheat pastry or 1/2 wheat and 1/2 unbleached)

Heat the milk and melt the butter in it. While this is cooling dissolve the yeast and the 1 tablespoon of honey in the warm water. When the milk has cooled, add the yeast-honey mixture to it. Stir them together and add the eggs, beating them in one at a time. Measure the flour into another bowl. Add the salt, spices and the rest of the honey. Add the flour 1 cup at a time, mixing well. When the flour is well mixed turn the dough out onto a floured breadboard and knead until smooth and elastic. Put the dough into a greased bowl, cover, and let rise in a warm place until double. Punch the dough down and turn it out onto the breadboard again. Separate into three equal parts. Take each of these parts, in turn, and begin rolling them with both hands on the board into long "snakes." Make them all the same size, or close to it. Lay them out on a large, round greased baking sheet (I use a pizza pan). Now braid them loosely and work the braid around until it forms a circle. Join the ends together, gluing them with a little water. Insert colored, hard-boiled eggs into the loops of the braid (some or all loops, depending on the amount of eggs available). Allow to rise again until nearly doubled. Paint the loaf with beaten egg white, then bake at 350 degrees for 25 minutes.

Makes one very large, beautiful loaf.

SPRING GREENS

If you are sure you can identify the wild greens of springtime, go gathering! Dandelion, watercress, sorrel, miner's lettuce, stinging nettle and many others are available in the spring (early or late depending upon your local climate).

Nature's wisdom provides for us exactly what our bodies and spirits need at this time of year. These spring greens stimulate liver activity, assist digestion and are rich sources of a multitude of vitamins and minerals necessary to help us resurrect ourselves into spring.

Serve them steamed as greens, shredded into salads, steeped as tea or drop them into a pot of your favorite homemade soup.

FAMILY EOSTRE RITUAL

If you live in a warm climate, you may want to hold the following ritual outside (in your garden even!), and walk the bounds of the garden as you do the chant and bless the soil of the gardens as well as the seeds. The nature spirits will appreciate this. They will also appreciate properly prepared soil and a good mulch.

Needed: a tall white candle, cauldron, a plate with some seeds for planting, some pots prepared with soil for planting the seeds, some water to water the newly planted seeds, usual altar equipment.

PRIEST:

> We celebrate this day the awakening of the Earth from her winter slumbers.
> The maiden has returned from the dark underworld, and life springs forth anew throughout the land.

PRIESTESS:

> Light and Dark stand as equals on this day.
> As the days begin to grow longer, brighter, warmer
> Let us celebrate the return of Spring
> With joy in our hearts and a song on our lips.
> Let us call upon the Magic Spirits of Spring!

EAST:

> Spring is the time for:
> Gentle breezes that turn into kite flying winds.
> Spirits of Air,
> Be with us now.

SOUTH:

> Spring is the time for:
> The balmy warmth of the sun on our backs as we plant things in our gardens
> Spirits of Fire,
> Be with us now.

WEST:

> Spring is the time for:

Spring showers to water our gardens,
Watching the birds bathe in puddles.
Spirits of Water,
Be with us now

NORTH:

Spring is the time for:
Working the good, dark, moist soil,
Finding earthworms, planting seeds
Admiring the first wildflowers.
Spirits of Earth,
Be with us now.

PRIESTESS:

Joyous Maiden, newly returned to Mid-Earth,
We see and feel your presence all around us.
We give greetings to you!

PRIEST:

Green Man! Lord of the Greenwood!
Shepherd of all creatures wild and free,
We see and feel you in all the newborn creatures of the wild.
We give greetings to you!

Priestess lights the tall white candle that is in the cauldron.

PRIESTESS:

We light this fire
On this day of equal light and equal dark,
As a symbol of the growing power of the sun.
May the cold darkness of winter be banished!
Let the light shine forth!

PRIEST:

Join with me as we call upon
The returning tide of light, life and growth!

We call forth the Gentle Rains!
Bless us, O Gentle Rains!
We call forth the Fertile Earth!
Bless us, O Fertile Earth!
We call forth the Warm Sun!
Bless us, O Warm Sun!
We call forth the Soft Breezes!
Bless us, O Soft Breezes!
Come forth, Springtime Powers of the Four Directions!

Come forth and bring bounty to the land!

All join hands and circle around the cauldron.

ALL:

Hail Earth, Mother of All!

All circle until Priestess calls "Down!" Then all drop to their knees, facing the altar, and channel the power raised into the seeds on the altar.

PRIESTESS:

Let the power stream forth through our hands
And into these seeds before us,
Symbolic of all the seeds
That will be planted in this season of spring.
Let them be charged with our energy,
And that of the Gods,
That with the protection and help
Of the nature spirits and devas,
They may grow strong and true,
Vibrant and healthy
So mote it be!

When all the power has gone into the seeds, the participants drop their hands into their laps, and a child, previously chosen, comes foreward and plants the seed or seeds in the prepared pots.

PRIEST:

Let us now bid farewell to the magic spirits.

EAST:

Spirits of Air, winds that blow free,
We thank you for your presence,
And now bid you farewell.

SOUTH:

Spirits of Fire, warmth of the sun,
We thank you for your presence,
And now bid you farewell.

WEST:

Spirits of Water, gentle spring rains,
We thank you for your presence,
And now bid you farewell.

NORTH:

Spirits of Earth,
Fertile, nurturing body of the Mother,

Devas, Nature spirits,
We thank you for your presence,
And now bid you farewell.

PRIESTESS:

Joyous Maiden, Gracious Mother,
Your presence is all around us.
We thank you.

PRIEST:

Lord of the Wildwood, Father of All,
Your presence is all around us.
We thank you.

PRIESTESS:

This rite is ended. Merry meet and merry part!

ALL:

And merry meet again!

MUSIC

PAN IN SPRING

1. Goat herds watch your herds to-night, Keep sharp your guard in pale moon-light
2. In the sec - ret plac - es where the   wolf kind pri - vate coun - cil share

Wolves are hun - gry in the spring for nan - nys fresh and old ones
Watch - ful in their wait - ing hours un - til the day is   fad - ed

Keep the need fire hot and dry un - til the sun is   ris - ing high
Goat herds hear - ing howl-ing songs some pack has run the whole night long

Hear them howl-ing in the moon-light call - ing to   their pack mates So
Emp - ty bel - lies mak - ing friends of all who would be fed now

cry   to Pan for all your flock, Leave milk and cheese up - on his rock. The

of - fer - ings ac - cep - ted still in pay - ment for good - will

Goat herds watch your herds to-night, Keep sharp your guard in pale moon-light
In the sec - ret plac - es where the wolf kind pri - vate coun - cil share

Wolves are hun - gry in the spring for nan - nys fresh and old ones
Watch - ful in their wait - ing hours un - til the day is fad - ed

3. Deep within remember, man, Where dwells the great and goatfoot Pan,
   Keeper of your herd from ill And blessing on your high hill.
   Keep in memory his flute, From which his music resolute,
   Draws your body and your blood You'll lay with him till morning.

4. So cry to Pan for all your flock, Leave milk and cheese upon his rock,
   The offering's accepted still In payment for good will.
   Deep within remember, man, Where dwells the great and goatfoot Pan,
   Keeper of your herd from ill And blessing on your high hill.

LURAILE

1. Dance in the dusk a__-wait-ing the moon Mist in the
2. Touch in the dusk with the La-dy a-bove Ris-ing her

eve, be__-fore night is quick-en-ing Old-er than moun-tains
eyes from her slum-ber-ing wak-en-in Young-er than kiss-es

Old-er than rune Dance in the name of the La-dy of Spring
sto-len in love

Lu-ra-lu lu-ra-lu lu-ra-i lu-ra-lu lu-ra-lu

lu-ra-lu lu-ra-i-le lu-ra-lu lu-ra-lu lu-ra-i

lu-ra-lu lu-ra-lu lu-ra-lu lu-ra-i-le

3. Child in the darkness, child of the night,
   Child of the firefly, flickering, flickering.
   Old as the horned one, young as delight,
   Dance in the name of the Lady of Spring.

4. Sweet as the touch from a soft petaled rose,
   Evening comes and the moon rises silvering.
   Sharing ourselves in the Lady's sweet bow'r.
   Dance in the name of the Lady of Spring.

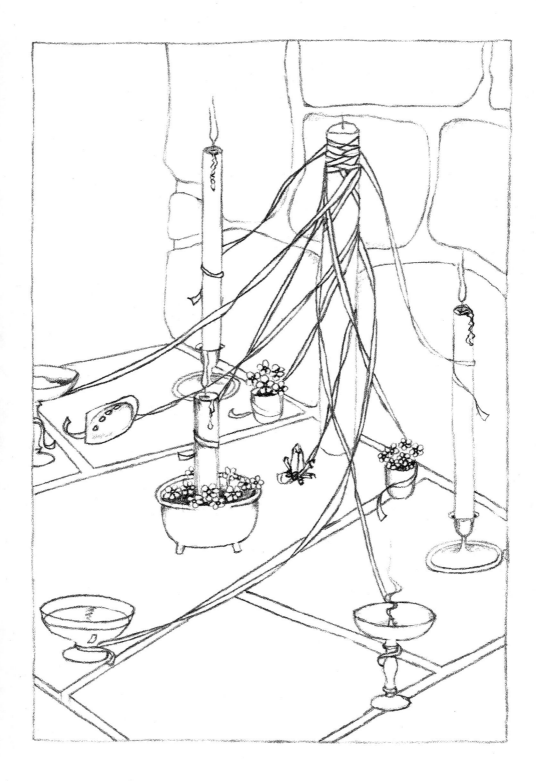

CHAPTER 9

BELTANE

May 1st

Hurray, Hurray, the first of May!

Ah, Beltane! Beautiful May Day! In most areas spring is in full flower now; the weather is beautiful and mildly warm. I must admit I've always been partial to the first of May—it's my birthday!

Beltane was celebrated in the ancient Celtic lands as the beginning of summer, just as Samhain, half way across the year, was the beginning of winter. On both occasions, the veil between the worlds was said to be thin, and it was no more unusual to see the fairies near Beltane than it was to see the spirits of the dead at Samhain. In Roman tradition, this day was called Floralia. It was a celebration of nature's blossoming and flower offerings were given to rivers and springs. It was sacred to Flora, the goddess of spring, whose very name translates to "Flower." Spring or summer, May Day tells us that the warm weather has arrived! The energy of spring has reached its peak; flowers can be found everywhere! The custom of having a young maiden as May Queen dates from long ago, as the May Queen is representative of the goddess of spring: Flora, Persephone, or whatever name you are most comfortable calling her.

In ancient times Bel-fires were lit on hilltops to celebrate the return of life and fertility to the world. Bel-fires had many marvelous virtues ascribed to them, as did all need-fires. Jumping over the fire could ensure safe delivery of a pregnant woman, bring spouses to young people, grant travelers a safe journey, ensure health, and bring about conception for a barren woman. If it is impossible to build a Bel-fire for your celebration, a tall red or white or yellow candle in a cauldron can be representative of it. Jumping the Bel-fire or candle should be done carefully (see the next chapter).

TRADITIONAL CUSTOMS

There are many charming Beltane customs. When my aunt was a girl in Canada many years ago it was customary for the children to go out early in the morning of May 1st and collect flowers, put them in baskets, and set them on the porches of friends and neighbors as a surprise. Perhaps this old custom is related to the custom of leaving bouquets of flowers out for the fairies. This was also done at Litha.

In parts of England and also in Scotland men would gather early Beltane morning and dig a large circular trench with a raised area in the middle. They would bring ale, beer and a somewhat custard-like oat dish called caudle, and celebrate Beltane. The drinks were passed around and the caudle was eaten. The caudle had knoblike protuberances which were pulled off and thrown over the shoulder, making wishes such as: "May the crows stay far from my corn." According to some scholars, partaking of the caudle originally had a far more serious meaning: one piece of it was secretly marked with charcoal and the person choosing it thereby became the "devoted one," scapegoat, or ceremonial victim of the Bel-fire, giving his life in sacrifice to the gods that the rest of the tribe might prosper.

> The fair maid, who, the first of May,
> Goes to the fields at break of day,
> And washes in the dew from the hawthorn tree,
> Will ever after handsome be.
> *Mother Goose*

As noted from the above bit of folklore, another May custom involves young maidens going out in the early morning and washing their faces with dew. This ensured them a beautiful complexion for the year, it was believed. In addition, it was said, they would marry the first man they met thereafter.

In Padstow, Cornwall, there is to this day a May morning procession involving an "Obby Oss." The Obby Oss, or hobby horse, seems an obvious symbol of male power, or perhaps it is the echo of an ancient Celtic Kingship custom involving ritual mating of the king with the Totem Horse Goddess of the tribe.

In Helston, Cornwall, on May 8th, there is a celebration known as Furry Day. This rather odd name comes from an old Celtic or Middle English word meaning "a holiday, fair or festival." Like May Day, it celebrates the end of winter and the beginning of summer.

Past accounts of the celebration tell that the inhabitants of the town spent the two or three weeks prior to Furry Day cleaning, painting, and sprucing up their homes and gardens. On May 1st there was a sort of preliminary observance. The town band played traditional music and the children danced spontaneously around the town. On May 8th, the town's buildings were decorated with flowers and greenery, the church bells were rung, and at 7:00 A.M. the dancing began. Young people danced at 7:00 A.M., school children at 10:00 A.M., the Mayor and well-dressed older couples at noon, and at 5:00 P.M. young people led a dance that all could join in. While some of the young people were dancing at 7:00 A.M., others were out in the woods gathering greenery and singing "Hal-an-tow" (given below in the music section). The noon dancers danced through all the main streets, into houses, and out again, to bring in summer and drive out winter.

ACTIVITIES

MAKING A MAYPOLE

The May Day custom we are most familiar with is the Maypole. Last year our good friend Michael came to our forested acres with his two sons and searched until he found a tall, thin tree, toppled by the wind. He took it home, removed the bark and lightly sanded it. He and his wife, Debbie, then made it a flower crown, attached long colorful ribbons, dug a deep hole in the back yard for it and voila—Maypole! The whole operation took about half a day.

Our local pagan community met at their house for a Beltane celebration. We performed a Maypole dance and some of the group also did Morris dancing while others played harps, guitars, fiddles and banjos, and we ended it with a marvelous salmon barbecue. The salmon was freshly caught from our local waters and whole when purchased. Our prayers and thanks to that salmon formed an integral part of our day's ritual.

If it is impossible to make a large Maypole, the children can help you make a small tabletop one. Use a cardboard tube, such as is found inside of paper towels, tinfoil or wrapping paper. Paint it pretty colors and attach strips of crepe paper to the top with glue. You can also glue some dried flowers on to the top, or make a tiny wreath with some fresh ones that fits exactly on the tube. When you are finished, carefully plant the pole into a pot of sand, inserting the bottom deep enough so that the pole will stay upright. This same procedure can be used to create a Maypole for a cake, using a piece of wooden dowelling for the pole and strips of ribbon for the streamers, and inserting into the center of the cake.

FLOWER CROWNS

Flower crowns are traditionally worn on Beltane by children and adults alike. The making of these can form part of the activities for your Beltane party. Green florists' wire is very helpful in this operation, but if you are unable to obtain it, the twist ties available at grocery stores for closing up plastic bags can be used instead. The procedure is fairly simple:

1) Use a pliable, thin piece of branch (such as ivy) and form a circle the size you want the crown, fitting it to the head of the person for whom it is intended. Wrap the ends with the florist's wire to hold them together.

2) Lay some of the flowers against the circlet and wrap the florist's wire around the stems, up to the blossom.

3) Continue to add flowers, fragrant herbs, leaves, whatever, affixing them to the crown by wrapping the stems with wire, until the entire circlet has been covered.

4) Long colorful ribbons can be attached to complete the crown.

This is one of those techniques that simply must be worked with to really understand how to do it. I must admit I haven't got the hang of it yet, but my teenaged daughter does a beautiful job.

PRESSED FLOWERS

From this point in the year and for several more months, flowers and herbs will be widely available for use in craft activities. Using a couple of heavy books and some blotting paper you can create a flower press and preserve some of the flowers and leaves for later use or study. A flower press will work for the delicate blossoms and rose petals, but to dry larger blossoms such as roses, you will need to have a drying box. Find a box just large enough to contain your flowers. Pour in a layer of cornmeal mixed with borax. Lay the flowers out taking care not to let them touch each other. Sift the cornmeal mixture slowly and gently over the blossoms until they are covered. Let them remain in the box about five days or so. Check to see if they are dry by gently uncovering a petal and touching it. If there is still moisture let the box sit another two or three days.

Herbs can be harvested (always with proper warning, prayers, and the permission of the plant) to use in potpourris, bath bags and other herbcrafts.

RECIPES

MAIBOWLE

1 quart white wine (or white grape juice)
1/2 cup brandy
sprigs of woodruff

strawberries
ice

In a punch bowl combine the white wine and brandy (omit brandy if you are making the nonalcoholic version). Rinse the sprigs of sweet woodruff and add them to the bowl, cutting them just before the flowers have opened.

Let sit for one hour and add the strawberries. Wild strawberries are best but even frozen, thawed ones will do. Add ice and serve.

BANNOCKS

1 cup rolled oats
1–1 1/2 cups oat flour
1/2 cup unbleached flour
1/4 teaspoon salt
1/4 cup oil or soft butter
1/2 cup warm water
1/2 teaspoon cinnamon (optional)

Stir together dry ingredients. Cut in butter or pour in oil and stir with a fork. Mix in warm water. Add more flour if necessary until mixture becomes a dough. Knead a little. Roll with rolling pin to 1/2 inch thickness and cut into rounds with biscuit cutter (a drinking glass can be used), and place on baking sheet. Bake in preheated 400 degree oven for 20 minutes.

CAUDLE

This tastes wonderful, as is, on Beltane morning. Modern palates, used to sweet things, might enjoy a dash of sweetener and vanilla on it.

1 cup oats
2 cups milk
1/4 teaspoon salt
2 eggs, beaten
2 tablespoons butter
1 teaspoon vanilla (optional)
2 tablespoons honey (optional)

Measure the milk and salt into a saucepan and heat slowly. Allow it to come to a simmer, not a boil, before stirring in the oats. Simmer for 6–7 minutes. In a small bowl, beat the eggs until yolks and white are well mixed together. Add 1 tablespoon of the cooked oats to the eggs and mix. Then slowly mix in an additional 2 tablespoons oats. Now slowly pour this mixture into the oatmeal, stirring constantly. Turn off the heat. Add 2 tablespoons butter and, if desired, the sugar and vanilla. Enjoy as part of a Beltane morning ceremony. Offer some of this as a libation to the earth, and you will be performing a ceremony of your Celtic ancestors.

FAMILY BELTANE RITUAL

This Beltane play/ritual celebrates the growing power of the light over the darkness, as well as the joining of will and action that must precede the act of creation. Bel is one of the old Celtic names for the Lord of Light. This play was written for a Beltane handfasting by Dancers of the Mist Coven.

The ritual area should be outside and marked out with sprays of flowers, branchlets, ivy, etc. This play requires twelve characters: Narrator, Priest, Priestess, Brigit, Bel, Two Monsters, a Drummer, and four people to summon the quarters. Two rather tall people are needed to escort Brigit into the circle and hold up her enclosure. The Narrator begins things by gathering the observers into a circle with his summoning chant.

Brigit should be dressed in a long gown of red, yellow, orange or variants thereof. Bel should also be wearing sun-colored clothing, or at least a shirt of that color. The monsters should be wearing black and situated on a black blanket or sheet in the exact center of the circle. Their clothes should be ragged, their hair unkempt.

Props needed are: a green cape and flower crown for Brigit, a yellow cape (with or without a sun face on it) for Bel, a hula hoop from which sheets have been draped to form a curtained enclosure for Brigid, a drum, a cauldron with a candle in it placed near the South end of the circle, and an altar with the usual items in the North end of the circle. Pan Pipes and a wooden spear are needed for Bel.

When all is in readiness, the Narrator takes the hand of the person closest to him (or her) and begins the chant. They begin walking and gathering people as they go, traveling in a circle or spiral, around and out again and finally forming a circle around the boundaries previously marked out.

Drumming begins.

NARRATOR:
> Haste! Haste!
> No time to wait!
> We're off to the Sabbat,
> So don't be late!

When all are formed into a circle, Priest and Priestess enter from the East. They stand by the altar. All is quiet for a few moments, then:

PRIESTESS:
> In the names above all names,
> And by the power of the Great Mother
> And her Mighty Lord,
> I cast out all influences and seeds of evil.

I lay upon them the spell of power and holiness
That they be bound fast as with chains
And cast into outer darkness,
And bother not the servants of the gods.

Priest and Priestess bless the elements.

PRIEST & PRIESTESS:
Creatures of Earth, Air, Fire and Water,
We bless you in the name of the Great Mother
That you may be of aid to us.

The Priestess and Priest go around the outside boundary of the circle, sprinkling and censing it.
Now two children go around the circle, one bearing the salted water, the other bearing a censer of incense, and sprinkle and cense the participants.
The elements are returned to the altar and all return to their places.

PRIEST:
Let the dwellers of far kingdoms be hailed!

NORTH:
Northern realms! Land of the Gnomes,
Spirits of the Earth, of the field, mountain and cave;
We summon you, lend of your strength.
We invite you to our Beltane rite.
Come! We bid you welcome!

EAST:
Eastern realms! Land of the Sylphs,
Spirits of the Air, of winds, storm and whirlwinds;
We summon you, lend of your wisdom.
We invite you to our Beltane rite.
Come! We bid you welcome!

SOUTH:
Southern realms! Land of the Salamanders,
Spirits of the Fire, of blazing heat and burning light;
We summon you, lend of your passion.
We invite you to our Beltane rite.
Come! We bid you welcome!

WEST:
Western realms! Land of the Undines,
Spirits of the Water, of sea, river and raindrop;
We summon you, lend of your gentleness.
We invite you to our Beltane rite.

Come! We bid you welcome.

Now all may be seated. Then the Narrator begins the tale.

NARRATOR:
>There was a time
>When the earth did not live as she now does.
>What is now our home was but a great, writhing, formless pit.
>And in this pit, fires raged endlessly
>And unthinkable monsters held sway.

Monsters, who heretofore have been seated motionless on the black blanket, now come to life. They begin snarling, making rude noises, wrestling and hairpulling with each other. They continue this, as appropriate, throughout.

>For where we now stand was once the pit of chaos. *(Drum beats wildly.)*
>And across the starry void, in the land of the Gods,
>Much was said of subduing the pit of chaos,
>But none succeeded.

The drumming now takes on a processional tempo as Brigit and her escorts march into the circle. The escorts are holding the draped enclosure and Brigit is within.

>And then stepped forward The Lady Brigit.

Hula hoop is dropped and Brigit steps out of it.

NORTH, SOUTH, EAST, WEST and ESCORTS:
>Brigit, Strong Mother, Eldest Guardian!
>Thy beauty gains fame with each passing day!
>Shining were thou when Romulus was a pup,
>Brilliant thy countenance now!
>Without thee, nothing can be born,
>Without thee, nothing can be made whole.
>The flame of life is thine.

Escorts place Brigit's cape on her.

NARRATOR:
>Brigit looked on the pit of chaos
>And knew she must choose her champion wisely.

Bel now begins to play the Pan Pipes (or whistle) as Brigit walks slowly around the circle looking appraisingly at all of the males. She shakes her head "No" at each one, until finally she comes to Bel. She looks at him for a while and nods "Yes," then points to him:

BRIGIT:
> You!

He looks surprised, points to himself, then follows her to the center of the circle.

NARRATOR:
> Thus did Bel volunteer
> To champion the Goddess Brigit.

Brigit ties the cape around his shoulders.

NORTH, SOUTH, EAST, WEST and ESCORTS:
> Lord of Beauty, Lord of Light,
> Lord of Regal Bearing Bright!
> Let us see you, let us hear you,
> Bring forth now your gracious might.
> Come to us now, find us here,
> We who seek you call you near.
> Boldly, brightly,
> Step now forth with shining spear.

Monsters make menacing noises and movements.

BRIGIT:
> Look on those pests!
> Look at this place!
> A disgrace it is,
> That fire should so wantonly rage,
> That nothing is formed,
> But that it is destroyed
> Before it may ever grow.

BEL:
> It is a disgrace!
> The only light shed by these flames
> Is the dark glow of foreboding.
> It is terrible to see the brilliance of fire
> In such destruction.

She hands him the spear; he just stands there for a minute and she gives him a not too gentle prod.

BEL:
> Into the fray!

He jumps into the chaos with spear and begins fighting. He slips and stumbles; the monsters definitely have the upper hand. They swat him, knock him over, sit on him, pull his hair, etc.

NARRATOR:
> But Bel could gain no footing
> In the fiery pit.
> For all was without form
> There was no firm ground on which to stand.

Monsters continue to get the better of Bel.

> And then Brigit stepped forward,
> And knew that she must help.
> Brigit took from her own shoulders
> Her great green cloak,
> The most beautiful garment
> Ever seen by man or god.
> And without hesitation
> She threw her mantle
> Over the fiery abyss.

Brigid comes forth and spreads her mantle over the pit, aided by escorts, covering Bel and the monsters. Struggling is seen under the cape, then Bel emerges, having won. He grabs the still snarling but much subdued monsters by the ears or hair, walks them over and sets them down firmly among the crowd at the edge of the circle.

NARRATOR:
> And so with a foundation to fight from,
> Did Bel vanquish the creatures of the fiery pit.
> And the green mantle of Brigid
> Continued to spread,
> To surround and enfold us all.

Narrator gestures to grass and trees and earth.

> Thus did Brigit bend
> The destructive fires to her will.
> Granting us the flame with which we cook,
> And forge and celebrate.

Arm in arm Brigit and Bel walk over to cauldron and light the candle within. They watch the flame while the narrator speaks.

> And so were joined the Lady Brigit
> And the young God Bel in their undertaking.
> And thus was joined the ability, to the will,
> In order to contain the raging, formless fires of chaos.
> And from this union—
> Worlds are born!

Brigit and Bel, arm in arm, exit the circle to the South.

PRIEST:

> Lady Brigid, Lord Bel,
> We thank you for your presence among us,
> And the gifts you have given us—
> The green earth, the radiant sun
> And our lives!

PRIESTESS:

> Let us thank the dwellers of the far kingdoms
> And bid them farewell!

NORTH:

> Spirits of the Earth, Land of the Gnomes,
> We thank you for attending our rites
> And lending us your strength.
> Go now to your lovely realm.

EAST:

> Spirits of the Air, Land of the Sylphs,
> We thank you for attending our rites
> And lending us your wisdom.
> Go now to your lovely realm.

SOUTH:

> Spirits of the Fire, Land of the Salamanders,
> We thank you for attending our rites
> And lending us your passion.
> Go now to your lovely realm.

WEST:

> Spirits of the Water, Land of the Undines,
> We thank you for attending our rites
> And lending us your gentleness.
> Go now to your lovely realm.

NARRATOR:

> My story is now ended
> My tale has now been told.
> Of Lady Brigit and Lord Bel,
> And the days of old.
> So go your way remembering
> Our Lady's bright green cape
> Lord Bel's brilliance and his spear
> And how the world took shape!
> Blessed Be!

MUSIC

The actual ritual for Beltane is dancing around the Maypole, wearing flower crowns, appreciating the beauty of nature and having a rousing good time. Before the dance is begun, the circle area can be ritually swept with a special broom to signify the sweeping out of the old tide of life to make way for the new.

There are wonderful songs that can be sung at this time of year. I have given some of them below, but a trip to the library's music and or folklore section will probably turn up a wider selection.

THE MAYPOLE DANCE

traditional

NOW IS THE MONTH OF MAYING

Thomas Morley
(1557-1603)

1. Now is the month of May - ing, when mer-ry lads are
2. The Spring clad all in glad - ness, doth laugh at win - ter's

play - ing. Fa la la la la la la la la Fa la
sad - ness.

la la la la la. Each with his bon - ny
And to the bag - pipe's

lass, Up - on the green-y grass. Fa la la la la
sound The nymph's tread out their ground,

Fa la la la la la la la Fa la la la.

3. Fie then why sit we musing, youth's sweet delight refusing,
   Fa la la la la la la, Fa la la la la la la.
   Say, dainty nymphs, and speak, shall we play barley break?
   Fa la la la la la la, Fa la la la la la la.

SUMMER IS A COMIN' IN

traditional

Sum - mer is a com - in' in___ Loud-ly sing cuc - koo,

grow-eth seed and blow-eth mead and spring-eth wood a - new.   Sing Cuc -

koo!   E - we bleat-eth af - ter lamb, low'th af - ter calf the cow;

Bul - lock start - eth, buck to fern go'th Mer - ry sing cuc - koo!   Cuc - koo

Cuc - koo Well Sing-est thou Cuc-koo___ Nor cease thou ev - er now.

HAL-AN-TOW*

traditional

Rob - in Hood and Lit - tle John, They both are gone to Fair___, O, And

we will go to the mer-ry green-wood To see what they do there___, O, And

for to_____ chase, O, to chase the buck and doe.

Hal - an - tow, Jol - ly Rum - ble, O

For we___ are up as soon as a - ny day____, O, And

for to fetch the sum - mer home, The sum-mer and the May___, O, For

sum - mer is a come, O, And win - ter is a gone, O.

* Halan means calends (first of the month), tow means garland.

PETERBOROUGH MAY SONG

traditional

Good mor - row, lads and la - dies, It is the first of

May. We hope you'll view our gar - lands, They are so bright and

gay. To the green-woods we will go, To the green-woods

we will go, go, go, To the green-woods we will go.

2. This bunch of May it looks so gay, Before your door it stands;
    It is but a sprout but it's well spread out By the work of our Lord's hands.

3. The cuckoo sings in April, The cuckoo sings in May,
    The cuckoo sings in June, In July she flies away.

4. I'm very glad the spring has come, The sun shines out so bright;
    The little birds upon the trees Are singing for delight.

5. The roads are very dusty, Our shoes are very thin;
    We have a little money box To put our money in.

PADSTOW MAY SONG

traditional

1. U - nite and u - nite and let us all u - nite For
2. With the mer - ry ring, a - dieu the mer - ry Spring

summer is a - come in to - day And whi - ther we are
How hap-py is the

go - ing we___ all___ will u - nite In the mer - ry
little bird that___ mer - ri - ly doth sing

Mom - ing of___ May 5. O, where is St. George O,

where is he, O? He's out in his long boat All

on___ the salt___ seas, O 6. Up flies___ the kite

Down falls the lark O, Aunt Ur - su - la__ Bird-hood, She

had an old   yowe   And   she died in   her own park, O.

3. The young men of Padstow they might if they would
    For summer is a-come in today
    How happy is the little bird that merrily doth sing
    In the merry Morning of May

4. The young women of Padstow they might if they would
    For summer is a-come in today
    They might have made a garland with the white rose and the red
    In the merry Morning of May

*   Verses 5 & 6 are already in the music.

7. Rise up, Mr. _____ , and joy you betide
    For summer is a-come in today
    And bright is your bride that lies by your side
    In the merry Morning of May

8. Rise up, Mrs. _____ , and gold be your ring
    For summer is a-come in today
    And give to us a cup of ale the merrier we shall sing
    In the merry Morning of May

9. Rise up, Miss _____ , all out of your bed
    For summer is a-come in today
    Your chamber shall be strewed with the white rose and the red
    In the merry Morning of May

10. Rise up, Mr. _____ , I know you well and fine
    For summer is a-come in today
    You have a shilling in your purse and I wish it was in mine
    In the merry Morning of May

11. Rise up, Miss _____ , all in your gown of green
    For summer is a-come in today
    You are as fine a lady as wait upon the Queen
    In the merry Morning of May

12. Where are those young men that now here should dance?
    For summer is a-come in today
    Some they are in England and some they are in France
    In the merry Morning of May

13. Rise up, Mr. _____ , and reach me your hand
    For summer is a-come in today
    And you shall have a lively lass with a thousand pounds in hand
    In the merry Morning of May

14. Rise up, Miss _____ , and strew all your flowers

For summer is a-come in today
It is but a while ago since we have strewed ours
In the merry Morning of May

15. Rise up, Mr. _____, with your sword by your side
For summer is a-come in today
Your steed is in the stable awaiting for to ride
In the merry Morning of May

16. Now we fare you well and we bid you all good cheer
For summer is a-come in today
We'll call no more unto your house before another year
In the merry Morning of May

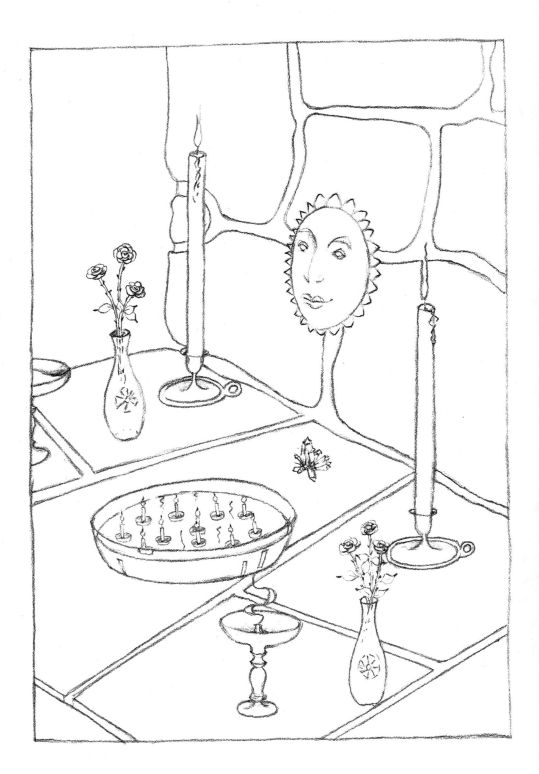

CHAPTER 10

LITHA

Summer Solstice - June 21st

Soon the battle's fought and the Holly King
Again will have his sway.

Litha is also referred to as the Summer Solstice and Midsummer. Christianity celebrates a similar feast a few days later and calls it St. John's Eve. There is much similarity in the way the two feasts are celebrated.

Litha marks the turning of the year from waxing to waning. The sun has reached its peak and now the downward trend begins. This day, like the winter solstice, is one when the sun seems to stand still. The next day it seems to move again, but the daylight hours are less than they were. It is a day of paradoxes: the sun has begun to die, the days grow shorter, yet the crops are still forming on the vine, the harvest is still ahead. Midsummer foreshadows the coming of winter, yet the hot weather of summertime is just beginning.

TRADITIONAL CUSTOMS

Many of the Midsummer customs that have come down to us have to do with fire, fertility and protection. Fire was seen as a purifying and sanctifying agent, capable of granting fertility and blessings.

It was customary to wear chaplets made of vervain and mugwort for this Sabbat, and to gaze at the Solstice bonfire through branches of larkspur. This was said to preserve the health of the eyes (though the vervain and mugwort, both said to increase psychic vision, were more likely used to enable one to see the fairies). At the end of the festival the herb chaplets were thrown into the fire and a request was made that all ill-luck would be burned up with the chaplets.

St. John's wort, with its bright yellow, sun-like flowers, was traditionally gathered at Midsummer. This powerfully magical and medicinal herb was used for both protection against evil spirits and, infused in oil, as a healing agent for burns.

Another custom of this time of year was a torchlight procession around the fields, to bless them and call them to the attention of the Divine Powers. Still another custom was the rolling of a burning wheel down a hill, in simulation of the sun's downward path. This one sounds rather dangerous in these modern times. However, the fire-wheel symbolism is valuable; keep it in mind when you are decorating. Maybe a vine wreath decorated with fire colored ribbons?

Many of the customs involving fire at this time of year were said to protect people from witches (I'll say no more about this one!), evil and disease, to grant fertility to humans and animals, and to illustrate the downward course of the sun from this time onward in the year. The bonfires and the smoke they produced were also thought to help the sun.

Speaking of fire-centered celebrations, think about the American Fourth of July observance. Traditionally celebrated with fireworks, it falls on the day which, according to the old style calendar (pre-1752), would have been St. John's Eve, June 23rd. This is the day when the Summer Solstice, which falls on June 21st or 22nd, was celebrated in most parts of Europe.

ACTIVITIES

Still another fire-related custom for Midsummer is divination by floating candles in a tub. This can be done at any Sabbat where divination is desired. To set this up requires a tub of some kind (we use the kids' plastic wading pool), foil-lined cupcake papers (walnut shells or the like can be used instead), a small amount of clay or play-dough, and some birthday candles. Put a piece of the clay big enough to anchor the candle into the center of each of the cupcake papers. Set the candles securely into the clay. They are now ready to use.

When it is dark outside bring out the candles on a decorative tray and set them near the tub. An adult or older child should be in charge of the matches. One by one let the children take up their "candle-cupcakes," make a wish and set them carefully into the wading pool, giving them a slight push to get them going. The divination is done by noticing how long the candle burns (how long it will take to come true), and which of the four (or eight) directions toward which it floats (the elemental influences that bear on the wish).

BONFIRE JUMPING

One of the customs for this day is the same as at Beltane—a need-fire. It is jumped also and for the same variety of reasons. The procedure for jumping a fire is something I'd better explain. When your fire is still new and small, use fireplace tongs or a stick to move one of the smaller pieces of firewood so that it sticks out to one side of the main fire. The small piece should be blazing, but the flames not very high. It is this small fire that can be jumped, being careful not to catch clothing on fire. Or you can make two small bonfires and run between them to collect on the luck of a need-fire.

TREASURE HUNT

A delightful activity for children for this sabbat is a treasure hunt. One year we made maps of our backyard wherein everyday things were given imaginative and mysterious names, i.e. the two mulberry trees became the enchanted grove, the small patch of herbs with a gravel path in the center became the winding way through the woods, etc. Clues can be given which lead the child to the next clue and finally to the treasure. The treasure can be anything you like. We made handmade Sun Medallions for our treasure, round wooden discs (they can also be made of bakeable clay), each painted a different color and emblazoned with a gold painted solar symbol in the center. A chart of solar symbols from various cultures is below.

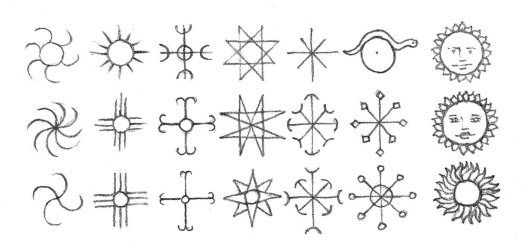

RECIPES

Recipes using leafy greens, early fruits and berries, the now plentiful supply of milk and eggs (especially noticeable if you own cows, goats, ducks or chickens) are good for this time of year.

I also like to make a round loaf of bread, using a French bread recipe, using small hunks of the dough to give it eyes, nose, mouth and rays. I call it my Sun God Bread. It can be made of two doughs, one light, one dark, swirled together a bit to represent the light and dark halves of the year.

SUN GOD BREAD

1 tablespoon butter
1 tablespoon sugar
1 tablespoon salt
2 cups boiling water
1 tablespoon dry yeast
2/3 cup lukewarm water
6-7 cups flour (1/2 whole wheat and 1/2 whole wheat pastry
    is a good combination, or perhaps 1/2 unbleached and 1/2 whole wheat)

Boil the water and pour it into a large mixing bowl. Add the salt, sugar and butter and stir until butter is melted. Sprinkle the yeast into the lukewarm water in a little bowl and allow it to dissolve. When the butter/salt/sugar mixture is lukewarm, add the yeast.

Add the flour one cup at a time and stir well. When the dough gets too thick to stir turn it out onto a floured bread board and knead it, adding more flour if necessary until it is smooth. Form it into a ball. Place it in a greased bowl, put in warm place, cover with a towel and allow to rise until double. Punch it down and let it rise again for about one hour.

Butter a large baking sheet. Remove a large piece of dough to use for later decoration of the loaf. Form the remaining dough into a nice round ball and place into the baking pan. Using the remaining dough, make little balls for eyes and nose, a longer, thin strip for the mouth, several long thin, rolled strips to be sunrays. Decorate the round loaf with these pieces. You may need a little water to help them stick on. Cover with a towel and allow to rise until double. Brush the dough with water. Then bake in a preheated 400 degree oven for about one hour. Remove and cool for a few minutes before carefully transferring loaf to serving platter.

The sunrays can be baked separately and placed around the round loaf as it sits on the platter. It is easier to keep the loaf intact this way.

FLOWER SALAD

Lettuce salad with borage, nasturtium and calendula petals sprinkled on top.

TAME AND WILD GREEN SALAD

Lettuce, etc., with comfrey, plantain, lamb's-quarters and other wild greens added.

DRAGON WING COOKIES

The Christian name for Summer Solstice time is St. John's Day. Another name for carob is St. John's bread, referring to St. John's survival in the wilderness on the fruit of the Honey Locust (carob) tree.

1/2 cup butter
1 cup ground almonds
1 teaspoon vanilla
1 cup brown sugar, packed
1 cup carob powder
1 cup flour
1 teaspoon baking powder
juice of one orange
2 teaspoons grated orange peel

Cream together sugar and butter. Add vanilla. Grind almonds in a blender and mix into butter/sugar. Mix in orange juice and orange peel. Combine flour, carob powder and baking powder and add slowly to creamed butter, stirring until well blended. Roll out on a lightly floured board to 3/4 inch thickness and cut with triangle shaped cookie cutter. Bake at 350 degrees for 11 minutes.

DILLED EGGS

6 eggs, hard cooked
1 teaspoon salt
1 teaspoon garlic powder
1 teaspoon dillweed
mayonnaise

Hard cook 6 eggs. Cool them quickly under cold running water then peel immediately for easy shell removal. Slice eggs in half. Put the yolks into a medium sized bowl and add the salt, garlic powder, dillweed and mayonnaise. Stir with a fork, crushing the yolks and mixing all together. Add enough mayonnaise to keep mixture from being crumbly. Spoon this mixture into the egg white "cups" and arrange on a serving platter. Chill and serve.

FAMILY LITHA RITUAL

This ritual is a play to be performed by children. It was written by Ed Fitch and me, and it celebrates the many aspects of summer.

Priestess wears flower wreath or crown and a cape, and carries a staff wound around with ivy and flowers. Hero is wreathed with green leaves and ivy, wears a helmet or crown, if desired, and carries a staff decorated with ribbons and fruit. He wears a green or blue cape. Wizard carries sword (and perhaps shield) for the Hero, and wears a cloak. Dragon is wreathed in yellow straw or a simulation thereof, wears serpent mask or helmet, and a brown or gray cape. He carries a sword. Magic Spirits wear elemental colored masks. Any other children who do not have parts can be involved in this ritual by joining the procession behind the Dragon. This ritual can be done inside or outside with the necessary modifications.

Procession with candles from outside in, or from a darkened room (if being done inside a house) or from inside a house to the outside ritual area, is led by the Wizard. He is followed by Hero, Priestess, and the Magic Spirits. The Dragon brings up the rear. As they walk they chant.

ALL:
>Green is gold,
>Fire is wet.
>Fortune's told,
>And Dragon's met.

As they reach the area of the ceremony, the children place the candles about the edge of the walls (safely please) or ritual area, and form themselves into a wide circle.

Priestess goes to middle of ritual area and raps with her staff upon the ground, then raises it.

PRIESTESS:
>We celebrate now the time of Midsummer,
>And call on the Magic Spirits
>To speak of this time.

AIR SPIRIT: (East)
>Summer is for running like the wind,
>And for being outdoors.

FIRE SPIRIT: (South)
>Summer is good and warm,
>When we live with the sun.

WATER SPIRIT: (West)
>Summer is for enjoying the water,
>Swimming, and watering the thirsty plants.

EARTH SPIRIT: (North)
>Summer is when the land is gold and brown,
>And will be that way until the rains come.

Hero goes to center, raps his staff upon the ground and holds it aloft.

HERO:
> Now is the time to enjoy the summer.
> School is out, and the days are long.
> It's fun to swim and travel,
> And to have the magic of playing and dancing
> In the night, and the moonlight.

Dragon bullies way to center, roars, hisses and looks around proudly.

DRAGON:
> This is my season!
> It's summer and it's hot!
> The grass is dying and there's no water.
> The air is hot, the ground burns your feet,
> The sun burns your skin,
> Makes you sweaty and dizzy.
> It's hot!

Wizard gives sword and shield to Hero and takes his staff.

WIZARD:
> To have a good summer
> And to enjoy our play,
> We have to defend ourselves and our land
> Against the Dragon.

Hero waves sword and slaps the Dragon with it.

HERO:
> Now you are going to get it!
> I have the magic sword of strength!

Dragon shrinks away even though he tries to fight back.

DRAGON:
> You can't beat me...
> This is my season!

HERO:
> I'll get you if it takes until the rains come!

DRAGON:
> It will!

They fight and the Dragon finally runs away.

PRIESTESS:

> Wait! Let us try to tame this Dragon
> And see if we can get it to do our bidding.
> All join hands and lets go after it!

They join hands, forming a long line, and run after the Dragon, finally catching up with it, encircling it.

PRIESTESS:

> Dragon, stay!
> Let us be friends!
> We need your light and heat!
> We need the power that summer brings!
> We need YOU!
> Let us be friends!

The Dragon turns cautiously around and faces them. He kneels at the feet of the Priestess.

DRAGON:

> For you, fair one, wise one,
> This I will do.
> While still keeping
> My unpredictable dragon nature,
> I will give to you of my light and heat,
> For the good of the earth and all her creatures.

ALL:

> Hurray for the summer Dragon!
> Blessed be the summer Dragon!

This is chanted three times, then the Dragon charges the line of children, breaks open the circle, and leads everyone to the refreshment table.

MUSIC

COME, FOLLOW

John Hilton
(1599 - 1657)

Come, fol - low, fol - low, fol - low, fol - low, fol - low, fol - low me!

Whi-ther shall I fol - low, fol - low, fol - low, whi-ther shall I fol - low, fol - low thee?

To the green-wood, to the green-wood, to the green-wood fol - low me!

LIGHT AND DARK

words and music
© 1992 Phillip Wayne

1. Light and dark leave their mark on each thing that grows be - low
2. Sum - mer king, flow - ers ring all the pla - ces that you know.

Dark will come, light will go, for each has their time I know.
You must go soon you know for your bro - ther's ice and snow.

3. Summer Queen, shoot and bean, All have flowered in your keep.
   Soon the white winter night Will let all the flowers sleep.

HEY HO, TO THE GREENWOOD

William Byrd
(1543 - 1623)

Hey   Ho   to   the   green - wood   now let   us

go!   Sing   Hey____   and   Ho!   And   there   shall   we

find   both   buck   and   doe!   Sing   Hey____   and

Ho!   The   hart   and   the   hind and the lit-tle pret___ - ty

roe!   Sing   Hey_____   and   Ho!

THE SUMMER KING

words and music
© 1993 Phillip Wayne

When sum-mer is come who__ wears the crown of green? On whose
When sum-mer is come, then the Green Man wears the crown. And the

should-ers is the ver-dant cape to be seen? Whose hands bear the
earth can wear the ver-dant cape all a-round. The Lord of the

staves of the i-vy, ash and thorn? And on what day was the lord of
Woods hold the i-vy, ash and thorn, And up-on the sol-stice was the

sum-mer born? View hal loo, view hal loo Ring the Sum-mer in the
sum-mer born.

Sum-mer in, Hal loo view hal loo Ring the Sum-mer in the Sum-mer in Hal

loo view hal loo, Ring the Sum-mer in the Sum-mer in, The Sum-mer King is

come to us we Ring the Sum-mer in.

THE HAYMAKER'S SONG

3. Here's nimble Ben and Tom, With pitchfork, and with rake;
    Here's Molly, Liz and Susan, Come here their hay to make.
    While sweet, jug, jug, jug! The nightingale doth sing,
    From morning unto even-song, As they are hay-making.

4. And when that bright day faded, And the sun was going down,
    There was a merry piper Approached from the town:
    He pulled out his pipe and tabor, So sweetly he did play,
    Which made all lay down their rakes, And leave off making hay.

5. Then joining in a dance, They jig it o'er the green;
   Though tired with their labor, No one less was seen.
   But sporting like some fairies, Their dance they did pursue,
   In leading up, and casting off, Till morning was in view.

6. And when that bright daylight, The morning it was come,
   They lay down and rested Till the rising of the sun:
   Till the rising of the sun, When the merry larks do sing,
   And each lad did rise and take his lass, And away to hay-making.

CHAPTER 11

LUGHNASADH

August 1st

"It seems wonderful to me
that the sun should rise in the west today
and in the east every other day, he said.
"It would be better for us if it were so," they said.
"It is the radiance of the face of Lugh of the Long Arms."

Lughnasadh is the feast of Lugh. Lugh (known as "Lugh of the Long Arms" and as "Lugh equally skilled in all the arts") was an Irish god of fire and light, associated with the sun and also with the grain. He is a type of god who loves the Great Mother, mates with her and dies (or is sacrificed) from this love, and is reborn. As such, he is related to, or perhaps an example of, the Oak King (God of the Waxing Year) who dies in battle with his own dark twin, the Holly King (God of the Waning Year). At Lughnasadh we commemorate Lugh's death by having a wake for him. Lugh's Oak King aspects are shown more clearly in the stories of his Welsh counterpart Llew Llaw Gyffes (the Lion with the Steady Hand). According to the Welsh tales, Llew was wed to Blodeuwedd, the flower maiden (obviously representative of the goddess of spring/summer). He was treacherously slain at Midsummer by Gronw, a rival for his wife's love. He is magically brought back to life to rule again, but before resuming his kingship, he first kills his murderer Gronw. An interesting aside to all this is to note that this festival of the Lion of the Steady Hand falls on August 1st, during the astrological month of Leo, whose symbol is the Lion.

Though at Lughnasadh the sun continues its decline in power as the days grow shorter, the grain has just been harvested. We give thanks for the grain and the spirit of the god represented by this grain.

In some traditions it is said that Lugh instituted this feast in honor of his foster mother Tailtiu.

Lughnasadh was an important event for the early Irish. The commemoration of Lugh lasted for about one month—two weeks before and two weeks after the actual date of August 1st. People came together from far and near to observe the event with fairs, games, contests, marriages and feasts.

The Anglo-Saxon form of this feast was called Lammas from *hlaf-mass* (loaf-mass), referring to the corn harvest and killing of the Corn King.

An activity that can be done at this time of the year is wheat weaving. My good friend, Morgyn Owens-Celli, wheat weaver par excellence, has graciously provided the following information to help you get started in this ancient craft. (See Activities below.)

In our family we celebrate this time of year by celebrating summer. Summer is heat, growth, abundance, and the work and play that naturally accompany these themes. Long hours of sunlight, tending our garden, harvesting fruits, vegetables, herbs, canning, freezing, drying our harvest—we celebrate summer with one eye on the winter ahead. We also find time to play: camping trips, beach picnics, nature walks, baseball games, children-produced drama or dance productions. Since two of our children have August birthdays, preparation for and celebration of birthdays are a major summer theme for us.

Summertime picnicking is an important event to us. What better way to appreciate what nature is offering us than to be outdoors as frequently as possible? After all, this is a nature religion! We try to plan a picnic every week of summer vacation. We vary the time of day, the location and the menu. Breakfast and dinner picnics can be an interesting change from the usual luncheon picnics. We are fortunate to be living in a location where both forests and the ocean are available to us, so many different types of outings are possible. The bounty of early summer is available at this time to be incorporated into our picnic menus: light, cool vegetable and/or pasta salads for hot days, vegetable/bean or meat soups and bread to keep us warm at our beach dinner picnics.

This is also the perfect time of the year to get that ice cream maker you've always longed for. Some are available at quite reasonable prices and even come with recipes. We've been known to have an "Ice Cream Social" type of a party, offering ice creams, sherbets (for the milk-allergic people among us), and a variety of toppings. A gathering like this can also be the occasion for a sing-a-long, and outdoor games such as croquet or horseshoes.

At this time of the year Mother Earth begins offering us some of the early fruits and vegetables. It is a time for canning, jam making, and other forms of food preservation. Have fun! And come winter, as you gaze upon the rows of home preserved foods, shining like colorful jewels on your pantry shelf, you will remember with fondness the warm, lazy, busy days of the summer just past.

ACTIVITIES

The following information on wheat weaving was written by Morgyn Owens-Celli. The designs, as well, are his creation.

WHEAT PREPARATION

There are a few things that you will need to know before you start your straw work. Wheat grows in the field with several series of leaves. Along the stem of the straw they separate the length into sections. The top section is what we will use for weaving. The other sections' straw is too thick to be used. The three important terms to remember are the ear or head (which is the carrier of the seeds); the nubs or neck (which is where the head connects to a section of undeveloped seeds); and the knee or joint (which is the section the leaf grows from). The section of straw between the last knee and the ear is the section that we use in wheat weaving. You will want to remove the lower sections of the straw and the leaf before it is ready to soak and work. The leaf is nature's way of keeping water off the straw during summer rains, but it inhibits the soaking of that section. The straw needs to be soaked in water (warm water speeds up the process). Some wheats require only fifteen minutes to soak and other varieties require four hours. You should always check with your supplier to see what they recommend. Most wheats require between one-half hour to an hour to soak. The thicker straw types require more soaking. The late varieties also require more soaking. Try soaking your wheat and pinching the very end of the straw. Does it spring back to your touch, or does it seem to resist or feel stiff? Remember that wheat is not at its best when oversoaked; it can turn a brassy yellow. Empty your water from the soaking tub and wrap the wheat in a moist towel. If you have soaked too much wheat for a weaving session, simply place it in a large plastic bag or in foil and freeze it. This maintains the moisture. When you remove it from the freezer rinse it off and wrap it in a moist towel.

MONMOUTHSHIRE MAIDENS

Monmouthshire Maidens are one of the most traditional historic designs in Welsh corn dollies. They are easy to spot because they are heart-like in shape. They are among the folk figures reminiscent of the ancient belief system in the various aspects of Mother Earth. In the spring, Mother Earth was believed to be young and maidenlike; she was as pure as snow and as innocent as the season. As the earth grew into summer, the Ancients believed her to be a mother figure as they saw the earth bursting forth toward the bounty of the harvest. As the earth bore her fruit and grew into the cold and depth of winter, they saw her as a crone, old in age and wise in experience. Their straw figures, created at certain times of the year, depicted this folk belief. Usually figures done in the spring were maiden in shape to represent that aspect. Some farmers in Wales would call the figures "tags" if they were made from grains harvested late and "maidens" if they were harvested early. Our Monmouthshire Maiden fits into the folklore of these figures. They are primitive in nature and earthy and textured in artistic simplicity.

To Make the Maiden

Make a column of nine very thick straws. Tie it just beyond the ears of wheat and three inches down from there. Now tie 18 straws. Secure them in some fashion so that you will be able to maintain tension and plait a hair braid. To do this, divide the 18 straws into three sections of six. Pull the right section over the middle section to lie inside the left section. Fold this left section over the middle (to form a right section) to the inside of the new right section. Alternate outside sections over the middle until you have woven nine inches. Tie off and set aside. Do a second side. Tie off and set aside. Now you will want to fasten them to the column. Attach each side to the column by tying on each side at the three inch mark from the ears. Bring up the plait curved to form the shape and tie up near the ears. Pull down the end of the plait and tie behind at the three inch mark. (See finished drawing for the description.) Fan out the wheat at the bottom to form her skirt.

To Make the Variation

To create the second Maiden, repeat all procedures as before with the exception of the final ties. Rather than tying the ends behind the three inch mark, cross them in front and tie them as seen in the picture.

* *

In order to make the herbal gifts we so love to make as Yuletide give-aways, we spend some time during the summer season finding flowers or herbs we can harvest and dry to make these lovely gifts. Lavender buds, rose petals and other colorful, fragrant flowers make beautiful bath bags, potpourris and sachets. Chamomile, red clover, nettles, comfrey, the mints—all these are a welcome addition to tea blends that we enjoy making for ourselves and others. These can be found growing wild even in many city locations. Make sure an area is unpolluted (not sprayed with insecticides, or too close to noxious automobile fumes) before you wildcraft any herbs.

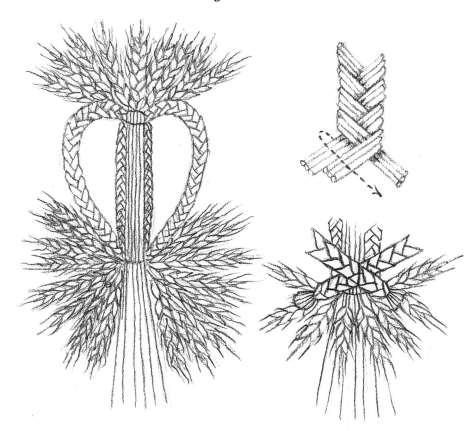

RECIPES

POTATO SALAD

10 medium size potatoes, cubed and cooked until tender
8 eggs, hard boiled, chopped
1/2 teaspoon salt (or to taste)
1 teaspoon dillweed
1 teaspoon minced garlic
1/4 cup minced green onion
1 large can black olives, sliced
2 stalks celery, chopped
1/2 cup (or more) mayonnaise

Place the cooked, chopped potatoes in a large bowl. Add the chopped eggs, celery and seasonings. Add in the sliced olives. Mix in as much mayonnaise as necessary to sufficiently moisten everything. Potato salad is usually served cold, but sometimes I serve it while everything is still warm and my family loves it this way.

VANILLA ICE CREAM

1 cup sugar
2 cups milk
1/2 teaspoon salt
6 egg yolks, beaten
1 1/2 tablespoons vanilla
2 cups heavy cream

Mix salt, sugar, milk and egg yolks in a heavy saucepan. Cook and stir over moderate heat until the mixture boils. Remove and immediately place the pan in cold water, making sure none of the water gets into the contents of the pan. Cool, and stir in the vanilla and the cream. Chill thoroughly and refrigerate 2-3 hours.

From this point on you will need to follow the instructions in the booklet that came with your ice cream freezer.

FRUIT TOPPINGS

These easy to make toppings can add interesting variety to vanilla ice cream. Fruits that can be used for this include peaches, nectarines, apricots, and any of the berries.

2-3 cups fruit, sliced or chopped
1/2 cup sugar or other sweetener

BARLEY WHEAT LOAF

A bread making machine is helpful with this recipe because the dough tends to be quite sticky. If you don't have such a machine, the recipe is worthwhile anyway; have some flour on hand to keep the dough manageable. Use as little flour as possible at this stage or the bread will be too dry.

3 cups hot water
2 tablespoons baking yeast
2 teaspoons salt
1/2 cup oil
1/2 cup honey
1 cup cooked barley
1 cup barley flour
1/2 cup gluten flour (optional)
7–8 cups bread flour

Measure the hot water into a large mixing bowl. Sprinkle the yeast over it, stir a little and let it rest for a few minutes until active and bubbly. Add the oil, honey and salt. Mix. Stir in the cup of cooked barley and mix well. Add the flour, in 2 cup increments, mixing with a spoon until the dough becomes too stiff. Turn out onto a floured board and knead in the rest of the flour. Knead for several minutes; the dough will become more manageable though still somewhat sticky. Place in an oiled bowl, cover and let rise until doubled. Shape into loaves and place into bread pans. Allow to rise again until doubled. Bake at 350 degrees for 30 minutes. Makes 3 loaves.

PESTO PASTA SALAD

8 ounce package of pasta
3-4 ounces of pesto sauce
1 large can black olives, sliced
1 large tomato sliced
grated parmesan cheese (optional)

The amounts here are only by way of suggestion. Everything here is done strictly to taste.

Use your favorite shaped pasta for this one. We use spiral shaped. Boil it according to the package directions, and drain. Put it in a bowl and add pesto sauce, sliced black olives and a chopped tomato. Add additional grated parmesan cheese if desired.

PESTO

1/4 -1/2 cup pine nuts (or cashews), ground up in the blender
2 teaspoons minced garlic
2-3 cups fresh basil, washed and chopped
1/2 cup olive oil
1/2 cup grated parmesan cheese

With the help of a blender, this recipe is no trouble at all!

Finely grind the nuts and pour them out into a small bowl. Put a cup of the basil into the blender, cover, and process at high speed. Add another cup of basil and process. At this point, add the garlic, and about 1/3 of the olive oil. Allow this to process until the basil pieces are quite small and well mixed with the other ingredients. Add the rest of the basil, some more oil and continue until the mixture's consistency is that of chunky peanut butter.

Add first the nuts, then the cheese, continuing to process. Add a bit more oil if necessary. The final product should be thick and pasty, with the basil chopped very fine.

Traditionally a pasta sauce, pesto is also good on potatoes, pizza, and can be dropped by tablespoonfuls into soup as a seasoning.

RAINBOW SALAD

2 carrots, grated
1 red beet, grated
1 yellow-orange beet, grated (these make the salad look so pretty
    they are worth the search)
1/8 of a red cabbage, thinly sliced
2-3 cups lettuce
a handful of spinach greens
1 cup sliced mushrooms

1/4 cup chopped green onions
alfalfa sprouts
borage flowers (these look beautiful as decorations on top of the salad
    and are deliciously edible)
any other raw vegetable you think should be in your salad

A basic oil and vinegar salad dressing goes well with this. One spiced up with herbs of your choice goes even better.

FRIED SQUASH FLOWERS

If you have a garden and are growing any kind of squashes, you will find you have an abundance of these beautiful flowers. They can be dipped in an egg batter, rolled in bread or cracker crumbs and deep fried.

FAMILY LAMMAS RITUAL

Our family celebrates this festival with a harvest dinner, the central feature of which is a freshly baked whole-grain loaf of bread. We use this opportunity to give thanks for that which has enabled our ancestors to live and for us to be.

The table should serve as the altar in this ritual and should be in the center of ritual area. It should be decorated as is appropriate to the season, with grain, fruits, corn, vegetables, leaves and flowers. The Lammas loaf and ale should occupy a prominent position on the table. The table should be in the center of the circle and have upon it vessels containing salt and water, a censer and some incense, two golden candles and symbols of the Lord and Lady. Use a harvest-type background music if desired.

The meal should include, in one form or another, the following food items: Fruit, vegetables, milk, bread, and ale.

The parents should serve as Priest and Priestess for this ritual, but all the other parts, except where noted, can be taken by the children and any guests present.

PRIESTESS:
      We gather now to celebrate the feast of Lammas,
      The feast of the first fruits of the Harvest.
      Our Mother Earth has blessed us with bounty,
      Our Father Sun has warmed and quickened the earth,
      The winds and the rains have come,
      And all have helped to nurture our crops to harvest.
      Let us be thankful on this day.

PRIEST:
      Let us give greetings

To the Magic Spirits of the four directions.

EAST:

Spirits of Air, bringers of the pollen bearing winds,
We greet you and bid you stay and feast with us.

SOUTH:

Spirits of Fire, bringers of the warmth
Of the summer sun,
We greet you and bid you stay and feast with us.

WEST:

Spirits of Water, bringers of the gentle rains,
Rains which water our thirsty crops,
We greet you and bid you stay and feast with us.

NORTH:

Spirits of Earth, you devas and nature spirits,
Caretakers and builders of the body of the Mother,
We greet you and bid you stay and feast with us.

PRIESTESS:

Bountiful Mother, we see your gifts all around us.
Generous Father, you have rendered the earth fruitful.
Without you both we would not be.
We give thanks to you and greetings,
And bid you stay and join in our merriment.

PRIEST:

Let us now celebrate the feast of Lammas!

All seat themselves at their places at the table. As each portion of the meal is blessed, the person blessing it shall extend his or her hands over it in attitude of blessing. After the blessing a small portion of the food is consumed in silence, while meditating on its significance.

PERSON#1:

Blessings be upon this fruit,
Earliest of the foods of our race.
Sweet and satisfying is this;
Gracious gift of the Lady and the Lord.
We give them thanks.

PERSON#2:

Blessings be upon these vegetables,
Colorful and wholesome offerings
To us from the plant kingdom;
Gracious gifts of the Lady and the Lord.

We give them thanks.

PERSON#3:

Blessings be upon this milk,
First food of all humans,
And of all our mammal relatives,
That which sustains new life.
Gracious gift of the Lady.
We give her thanks.

PERSON#4:

Blessings be upon this bread,
Embodiment of the Sun God's essence,
Each kernel of this grain forms a link
With one that has come before,
A chain extending back into time,
To our race's very beginning.
Eat of this bread,
And know that it is a link with our past
And a promise of all that shall come to be.
For this gracious gift of the Lady and the Lord,
We give them thanks.

PERSON#5:

Blessings be upon this ale,
The Sacred Alchemical Marriage of grain and herb
Brings into creation something new and unique.
By the One Power may we likewise be magically transformed.
For this gracious gift of the Lady and the Lord
We give them thanks.

PRIESTESS:

As we celebrate our ancient mysteries once again,
Let us give thanks to Earth and Sun
For the gifts of the fruits of their union.
And may the Old Gods bide with us
And grant us their blessings.

PRIEST:

Let us now complete our Lammas feast
With gratitude and love
For the source of our being.

ALL:

Blessed Be!

MUSIC

JOHN BARLEYCORN

traditional

1. There were three men came out of the west___ Their   for - tunes for to
2. They've plowed, they've sown, they've harrowed him in   Threw clods up - on his

try   And__ these three men made a so_-lemn_ vow John Bar-ley-corn must die
head   And__ these three men made a so_lemn_ vow John Bar-ley-corn was dead

3. They've let him lie for a very long time
   Til the rains from heaven did fall;
   And little Sir John's sprung up his head
   And so amazed them all.

4. They've let him stand til Midsummer's Day
   Til he looked both pale and wan.
   But little Sir John's he's grown a long beard
   And so become a man.

5. They've hired men with the scythes so sharp
   To cut him off at the knee,
   They've rolled him and tied him by the waist
   And they've served him barbarously.

6. They've hired men with the sharp pitchforks
   Who pricked him to the heart,
   And the loader he has served him worse than that
   For he's bound him to the cart.

7. They've wheeled him around and around the field
   Til they came unto a barn
   And there they made a solemn oath
   On poor John Barleycorn.

8. They've hired men with the crab tree sticks
   To cut him skin from the bone
   And the miller he has served him worse than that
   For he's ground him between two stones.

9. They've worked their will on John Barleycorn
    But he lived to tell the tale.
    And they pour him out of an old brown jug
    And call him home-brewed ale.

10. And little Sir John and the nut-brown bowl
    And he's brandy in the glass.
    And little Sir John and the nut-brown bowl
    Proved the strongest man at last.

11. The huntsman he can't hunt the fox
    Nor so loudly blow his horn
    And the tinker he can't mend kettle nor pots
    Without a little barleycorn.

LUGHNASADH DANCE

words and music
by Gwydion

1. Lugh, the light of sum - mer bright, Cloth - ed all_ in green,
2. Lugh, grew tall from spring to fall, Then sought to find a wife, But

Tail - ti - u, his moth - er true, Rise up and_ be seen
Ba - lor came and made his claim, And swore to take Lugh's life.

Chorus: At your fes - ti - val sounds the horn, Call-ing the peo-ple a - gain

Child of bar-ley corn, new - ly sum-mer born Rip-en-ing like the grain.

3. The two did fight from morn 'till night
   When Lugh did strike him one;
   Balor's eye flew in the sky
   And there became the sun.

4. Lugh was wed and made his bed
   With Erinn in the north,
   And there they lay for many a day
   And soon a child came forth.

5. The child grew tall from spring to fall,
   Setanta was his name,
   But then at length, by honor's strength,
   Cuchulain he became.

CHAPTER 12

MABON

Fall Equinox - September 22nd

The boughs do shake and bells do ring,
So merrily comes our harvest in,
Our harvest in, our harvest in,
So merrily comes our harvest in.

We've plowed, we've sowed,
We've reaped, we've mowed.
We've got our harvest in.

Mother Goose

Mabon, the Fall Equinox, or Harvest Home, as it is frequently referred to by pagans, is unquestionably a harvest festival. Whether or not any kind of harvest observances are held at Lughnasadh or Samhain, one is generally held at Mabon. So deeply rooted was the English tradition of a harvest festival at this time of year that the early Pilgrim settlers, having missed this important date to give thanks due to a late harvest, held a belated harvest festival anyway, when their crops were finally in, thus giving birth to the modern, late fall American Thanksgiving tradition.

It was traditional to have some sort of ceremony around the last sheaf of grain harvested. (In some places this activity was also carried out closer to Lughnasadh, depending on when the last on the grain was harvested.) In England, the last sheaf left standing was braided into a corn dolly and carried ceremonially to the harvest supper. This dolly represented all the elements needed for the next growing season. In other areas, whoever cut the last sheaf was considered to be killing the corn spirit and therefore bound to have bad luck. In order to dilute the bad luck all the workers would throw their sickles in turn so that all shared the responsibility of the last cut. They then made the corn dolly from the sheaf. The dolly was kept until the following year when it replaced by the new one. Making corn dollies especially for this purpose is a good activity for the Harvest season.

Harvest Home marks the completion of the second of the three harvests (the third one being Samhain). The gathering in of the crops has been accomplished (more or less, depending on your local growing season). It is a time for rest after labor, a time for enjoying the abundance and giving thanks for it.

In another sense, all these themes relate to us on a personal level. The spring and summer have been open, flowering, productive times of the year. At Harvest Home we see this part of the cycle ending. We have breathed out, now we must breathe in. We have labored and earned our reward, as well as our rest. It is time to rest for a bit and, after a while, begin to plan ahead for next growing season. The cold months ahead will force us to be more contracted, more inward. The light that has burned brightly in an outer sense during the spring and summer will now be burning brightly within us, as we have labored and prepared for these cold months on a spiritual as well as physical level.

What does this mean in terms of our everyday life? At the Fall Equinox we look ahead in time, and we see winter coming. The cold weather forces us to spend more time inside, physically, mentally, spiritually. We are more given to introspection, planning, sitting by the fire, and reading, as well as other inner-type activities. At this time of Equinox, winter has not arrived yet, but we see it coming, and we know that we have prepared for it, are still preparing for it in some ways. But the harvest is in, and physically a time of rest from hard labor has begun (unless you haven't begun chopping wood for the winter yet!).

Our family celebration of this Sabbat is always a feast, with as many friends as can join us. We do the ritual around our decorated table. We indulge in as much singing, dancing, and poetry of the season as is humanly possible.

ACTIVITIES

NECKLACES

To make bean necklaces use beans of your choice and soak them until they are able to be pierced by a needle. If you soak any longer they begin to split. Thread a needle with dental floss or other strong material and string the beans onto it. By using various kinds and colors of beans quite beautiful necklaces can be made.

Acorns and other nuts can also be used for making necklaces. Drill a hole large enough for a needle to pass through and string them as above. The same could be done with eucalyptus pods and whole, dried rosehips.

Nuts of various shapes can also be used to make little people. Use a large one for the body, smaller ones for head and limbs. Drill small holes and stick them together with toothpicks and glue. Cut a piece of felt in a triangular shape and sew it together to make a hat. Another piece of felt, cut in a rectangular shape can be gathered at the top with needle and thread to make a cloak for the little person. Features may be drawn on the face with a felt marker if desired. A bit of wool roving can be glued on for a beard, and a small twig stitched to the cloak for a staff.

Gnomes can be made be cutting a piece of felt into a T-shape (see illustration), sewing it together as indicated, and stuffing it with wool roving. Our children like to make these little wool people in yellow, red, blue and green to represent the four quarters for use on their personal altars.

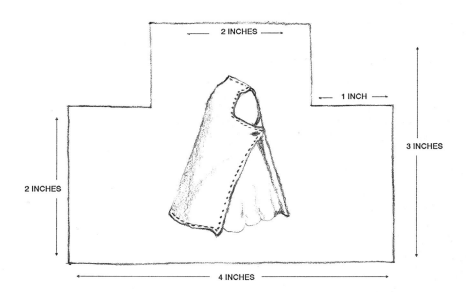

Lots of objects can be made from nut shells that separate easily into halves, such as walnut. Boats, gardens, baby cribs—all are easy to make. To make a boat, put a bit of clay in the base of the shell and add a toothpick to which has been glued a triangle of paper. To make a garden also use clay and stick into it tiny dried flowers. To make a crib, put into the shell a drop of glue followed by a small wad of wool. Tuck a small square of flannel into the shell. It is now ready for any tiny creature who wants to sleep in it.

Another good fall activity is making leaf rubbings. Put the chosen leaf under some paper with the ribbed underside of it turned upwards. Gently color over the paper covered leaf and its pattern will show up on the paper.

RECIPES

Our harvest dinner consists of baked squashes filled with wild rice, chopped apple and nuts, a green salad, a bean dish of some kind, cornbread, and homemade applesauce and a blackberry pie. Our ritual is done around the dinner table, loaded down with its splendid feast. We usually move the chairs out and stand around the table.

CORNBREAD

1 cup cornmeal
1 cup flour
1/2 teaspoon salt
2 teaspoons baking powder
1 egg
1/2 cup melted butter or margarine
1 cup milk
1/4 cup honey (or less to taste)

Melt butter, mix in milk and egg. Mix together dry ingredients. Add milk mixture to dry mixture and blend together. Stir in the honey. Bake in preheated 350 degree oven for 20 minutes or until a toothpick comes out clean.

BAKED SQUASH

1 medium to large winter squash
2 cups wild or brown rice
4 cups water
1 teaspoon salt
1 cup nuts
3 apples

Any of the orange, hard, winter squashes may be used. Put it into the oven at 350 degrees and bake for about 30 minutes. Cook the rice according to package directions (brown rice does nicely if you can't find wild rice, or mix the two for something unique). Chop the nuts and apples coarsely. Mix the cooked rice, nuts and apples together and stuff the half cooked squash. Put the squash into a pan, covered if possible, and cook for another 30 minutes or until the stuffing is hot and the squash is done.

BEANS

Cook up a pot of your favorite beans, spice them the way you like them or use our recipe:

3 cups black beans, cooked
1/2 cup lemon juice
3–4 teaspoons soy sauce
1 onion, chopped
2 cloves garlic, minced
3 tablespoons oil
1/2 teaspoon salt, or to taste
1 bunch chopped cilantro

Saute the onions and garlic in the oil. Mix into the cooked beans. Season with the lemon juice, soy sauce and salt. Use this method with either mashed or whole beans.

HOMEMADE APPLESAUCE

Use about 10–12 medium to large cooking apples. Core them and peel if desired. Chop them coarsely into 1/2 to 3/4 inch chunks. Put into a large pot and barely cover them with water or apple juice (apple juice makes the end product sweeter). Simmer until soft. Using a potato masher, mash until remaining juice is combined with apples (do not attempt to mash up all the chunks of apple). Serve as is, or seasoned with a few sprinkles of cinnamon. Good hot or cold.

FAMILY HARVEST RITUAL

Here is our family's Harvest Ceremony, held outside in the late afternoon (weather permitting) around a table filled with the season's bounty.

PRIEST:
> Family and friends, I bid you to link hands,
> For now, as in ancient times,
> We gather to give thanks
> For that which has been given to us
> by our generous Mother Earth.

PRIESTESS:
> This is a season of abundance and joy
> Worthy of celebration now as in times long past,
> Honoring Our Lady of the Harvest,
> The Mother Earth, Giver of life,
> Golden and beautiful in autumn,
> And Our Harvest Lord, the resplendent Sun King,
> Giver of Light, Laughter and Fertility.

PRIEST:
> Let us now call upon the Magic Spirits in a rite of thanksgiving!

EAST:
> Spirits of Air!
> You who dwell in the gentle winds
> That blow fresh and pure;
> We thank you for nurturing our crops to harvest.

SOUTH:
> Spirits of Fire!
> You who dwell in the brilliant warmth
> Of the fires of the sun;
> Giving of light, strength and cheer,
> We thank you for nurturing our crops to harvest.

WEST:
> Spirits of Water!
> You who dwell in the sparkling streams,
> Deep lakes and soft rains;
> Bringing refreshment, nurture and renewal,
> We thank you for nurturing our crops to harvest.

NORTH:
> Spirits of Earth!
> You who dwell in the fertile fields,
> Deep forests and high mountains;
> Bringing forth life, beauty and abundance,
> We thank you for nurturing our crops to harvest.

OLDEST CHILD:
> To the rain that has fallen,
> To the sun that has shone,
> To the farmer working in his field,
> To the wind that has blown;
> To the gentle, healing herbs,
> To the life within the seeds,
> We give our thanks for all your gifts,
> For meeting all our needs.

YOUNGEST CHILD:
> For the gift of one another,
> To the Sun so high above,
> To the Earth in all Her beauty,
> We offer up our love.

PRIESTESS *(All repeat after her, line by line):*
> For the bounty of the Harvest
> Do we give Thee thanks!

Blessed be the fires of Autumn!
Blessed be the harvest!
Hail Earth Mother of all!
Hail the Golden Sun!

Repeat the last two lines at least 13 times.

PRIESTESS:

At this time let us reflect upon and give thanks for
All that has sustained us, has helped us to live,
And helped sustain all those who lived before us—our ancestors.
Think of the animals who have gifted us with their bodies
That we might have food and clothing.
Think of the trees that have given of their bodies
That we might build our dwelling places.
Think of the seeds being gathered, then planted;
Think of crops growing;
And from those crops, more seeds, and more planting,
Down through the eons of time
So that we might be here today.

PRIEST:

Family and friends, this ritual is ended.
This is a time of joy and thanks,
So let us now, as we eat and drink,
Give thanks, within ourselves
For this bountiful season,
For each other,
And for all the richness of our lives.

Let the feast of harvest home begin!

MUSIC

COME, LITTLE LEAVES

George Cooper   unknown

1. "Come, lit-tle leaves," said the Wind one day, "Come o'er the meadows with
2. Soon as the leaves heard the Wind's loud call, Down they came flut-ter-ing,

me and play; Put on your dress-es of red and gold For
one and all; O - ver the brown fields they danced and flew, A -

sum____ - mer is gone and the days grow cold."
sing____ - ing the glad lit - tle songs they knew.

3. Dancing and whirling the little leaves went;
   Winter had called them, and they were content;
   Soon fast asleep in their earthy beds,
   The snow laid a coverlet over their heads.

HARVEST SONG

Unknown

Marlys Swinger

The boughs do shake and the bells do ring, So mer-ri-ly comes our

har - vest in, Our har - vest in, our har - vest in, So mer-ri-ly comes our

Fine

har - vest in. We have ploughed and we have sowed,

We have reaped and we have mowed, We have brought home ev - 'ry load,

D.S. al Fine

Hip, hip, hip, our har - vest home! The

HARVEST DANCE

words and music
by Gwydion

1. Don__ now the wreath of gold, and bear the torch - es in the_ cold
2. Old golds are stand-ing near, To watch the turn - ing of the_ year;

Thru the brown and bar - ren field, Where the fair-ies have trod.
Far from the for - est's gloom Fair - ies pipe_ their tune.

Press the lights in - to the soil And 'round the cir - cle writhe and_ coil;
Strong staves of row - an - tree Shall keep the mea-sure mer - ri__ - ly:

For the a - bun - dant yield Thanks be un - to the god.
Ash - branch and sprig - of - broom Flash be - neath__ the moon.

Bear the bask-ets filled with grain, Oats and bar - ley and rye;
Rise up and join the___ ring 'Round the har - vest - tide blaze:

Hide them from the pour-ing rain Soon to dark - en the sky.
Praise now the Wan-ing King In the last of his days.

'Round and a-round and a-round we go, Some-times fast and some-times slow;

'Round and a-round and a-round the ring of the Sum-mer born King.

3. Hand to hand we pass the blade Unsheathed by the Ivy Maid:
   Keen the edge that cuts the hand Of the dancer unwary.

   Greet the god with open arms And bind the rings with sylvan charms.
   Raise the spirits of the land. Sylph and naiad and fairy.

   Bear now the Maiden's blade To the altar of stone.
   Here where the god has stayed Till the harvest has grown.

4. 'Round, 'round, upon the ground, Where Jack O'Green is autumn-bound.
   Whirl, whirl the Ivy Girl, Where the harvest was springing.

   Bright, bright the firelight When day is turning into night:
   Swirl, swirl, the smoke doth curl. While the dancers are singing.

   Dance 'neath the Autumn Crown, 'Mongst the fardels and sheaves;
   Dance now upon the brown Branches, tendrils and leaves.

CHAPTER 13
MOONTIDES AND MAGIC

O Lady Moon, your horns point to the East:
Shine, be increased!
O Lady Moon, your horns point to the West:
Wane, be at rest!

(Christina Rossetti)

What is magic?

There are many definitions of magic, the one by Aleister Crowley is probably the most famous: "Magic is the science and art of causing change to occur in conformity with one's will." Another definition states that magic is the willed aspect of psychic activity. What they all seem to come down to is this: That by using whatever means that work for us, if we are able to focus our will intently on the desired goal, raise some energy or power and channel it toward our desired goal, we will be able to bring about changes in our lives.

There are many things available to us that can aid us in helping to focus our wills. Sensory aids are a great help to us all, excepting perhaps the most advanced adepti. Sensory aids include things like incense, music, chanting, crystals, visual aids such as colors or meaningful symbols, as well as totem plants and animals. Sensory aids can also include things that are processes, such as drawing a picture or symbol of the desired goals, and imbuing a candle or other object with power to be released in working towards the goal.

How does all this apply to children? Working magic with children can be a very fun and creative endeavor—they can really get involved in the process of "making magic." Ask your kids what kind of features they would like in their "dream house" and see what kind of response you get. Everyone will have ideas to contribute. By writing down or drawing their ideas they are focusing on them. By talking about how wonderful it would be to have two fireplaces or a bigger backyard, they are becoming excited—generating energy, in other words. Help them write a short poem about how wonderful it will be to live in this house. Do all this in a ritualistic setting with candles, chanting, incense and such and before you know it you'll have a new house!

Of course you all know I am oversimplifying the situation to make my point. We are not really trying to teach our children that every single thing they chant and burn candles for they will get. What we are trying to teach them is to put energy and effort towards what they truly want out of life. We also need to teach them that when we don't get exactly what we have worked magic for, that often it will come to us another way, or perhaps the universe has another plan and it would be better for us to get out of the way and let things flow.

When working magic there are at least two ways to deal with the energy you are raising. The energy can be channeled into the candle, or whatever object you have chosen to represent the person or goal of the magic. Then burn the candle or deal appropriately with the object (i.e. bury it in the earth, throw it in the ocean) to release the energy toward the desired goal. Another way is to visualize the energy going directly to the person or desired goal, without the use of an intermediary object such as a candle.

The moon, in her monthly course, presents us with three separate and distinct faces: new, full and dark. These correspond with the three aspects of the Goddess—Maiden, Mother and Crone. Looking at it from a slightly different view, the moon is said to be waxing as it grows from new to full, and waning as it shrinks from full to dark. So we really have five moon phases to use in planning our magical workings: new, waxing, full, waning, and dark.

From time immemorial people have been observant of the tides of the moon when working magic. As the light and power of the moon waxes and wanes throughout her phases, we gear our magic working accordingly. If much power is generated, successful magic can be worked regardless of the phase of the moon; but it has always made more sense to me to "go with the cosmic flow" in these matters.

As one would expect there are definite kinds of magical workings associated with the different phases of the moon.

The new moon is a time for workings associated with establishing goals, starting new projects, planting seeds (of all kinds) and initiating growth. In this context of new beginnings it is a good time for doing healing.

The waxing moon is a time for encouragement, construction and growth, for blessing and nurturing.

The full moon is a time to assess progress made on the above, to observe the fruition or lack of fruition of whatever was initiated at the new moon. It is a time for removing negatives and replacing them with positives. It is a time for doing rituals requiring a good jolt of power, for attracting things such as love, health, money. It is a time for nurturing and blessing. The full moon is also a time for psychic recharging.

The waning moon is a time for banishing the old and outworn, for again evaluating progress on our goals, and for beginning to think about new ones. It is a time for gradually drawing within. In the context of banishing the outworn, it is a good time for healings that involve releasing.

The dark moon is a time for making shields of protection around ourselves. It is a time for silence, inner visions, transformative dreams and otherworldly experiences. It is a very potent time, when the power of the Crone is predominant.

Moon rituals should also take into account the sign of the zodiac that the moon is in. A full moon in Scorpio will express differently than a full moon in Aries. Refer to the chart below for the energies and attributes of the signs of the zodiac. It will help you fine tune your magical working.

A magical goal can be approached from different angles during different phases of the Moon. For example, if you are desperately unhappy in a job and would like a change in the situation and the moon is waning, you could use the moon's energy to banish the elements that are causing you distress. If the Moon was dark, you might ask for a vision to help you see your way out of the difficulties. If the moon was new, you could work for a new and more positive development in your work place, perhaps even a new job. If the moon was full, you could work for psychic recharging and blessings to carry you through and enable you to withstand the pressures of your situation.

Make sure when you are doing magical workings of any kind that you state your goals and processes in a very concrete manner. After you have formulated your goals and expressed them concretely, do your ritual and see your goals as realized. Then release them to the universe to be taken care of.

Rituals held at moon tides can be very simple. We gather ourselves around the altar, cast a simple circle, evoke the powers of the four directions and the God and Goddess. We then do a short guided meditation relevant to the phase of the moon. For instance, at the dark moon the meditation could involve a visit with a wise, old grandmother for guidance on problems being experienced, or just to gain access to her wisdom. At the new moon, it could involve a visit with the Maiden for inspiration in our lives for the coming lunar cycle. At the full moon, it could be a visit with the Mother just to bask in her loving protection and nurturance, or perhaps to reassess goals in progress. It is wonderful just to sit in the light of the full moon and consciously drink in its power, let yourself be psychically recharged. A quartz crystal can be charged in the moonlight and brought inside to radiate its power during the remainder of the month. Another good full moon activity is to make Moon Water. Ritually bless a container of water, pour it into a glass jar, cover it and leave it out during the night to absorb the power of the full moon's rays. Whenever you need the special qualities of the full moon in that particular sign of the zodiac, drink a few drops of it in a prayerful, conscious manner.

After the guided meditation any healing or magic can be done. Finally the powers of the directions and the Deities should be thanked and bid farewell, and the circle dissolved.

SOME BASIC ASTROLOGICAL INFORMATION

SIGN	PLANET	KEYWORDS
Aries	Mars	emergence, initiating, pioneering, forceful, blunt, courageous
Taurus	Venus	rootedness, sustaining, practical, patient, charming, beautiful, stubborn, possessive
Gemini	Mercury	communicative, restless, versatile, witty, inquisitive, spontaneous, superficial, nervous
Cancer	Moon	inner sensitivity, emotional, imaginative, loving, protective, sympathetic, evasive, moody
Leo	Sun	creative, generous, enthusiastic, dignified, graceful, expansive, dramatic, dogmatic, proud
Virgo	Mercury	practical, meticulous, critical, finicky, analytical, discrimating, communicative, service oriented
Libra	Venus	harmonious, easy going, smoothly aggressive, romantic, diplomatic, idealistic, balance oriented
Scorpio	Mars	intense, emotional, persistent, determined
	Pluto	obstinate, subtle, deep feelings, suspicious, secretive

Sagittarius	Jupiter	aspiration, friendly, excitable, optimistic, philosophical, enthusiastic, sincere, jovial, arrogant, opportunistic
Capricorn	Saturn	reliable, cautious, prudent, ambitious, patient, persistent, rigid, structured
Aquarius	Uranus	original, inventive, unconventional, needs freedom, ingenious, progressive, friendly, humanitarian
Pisces	Neptune	mutable, sensitive, emotional, intuitive, compassionate, humble, vague, vacillating, careless

RECIPES

Here is my favorite all purpose cookie recipe, adaptable to dark moons by the addition of carob or chocolate powder.

FULL MOON COOKIES

1/2 cup butter or margarine
1 teaspoon vanilla extract
3/4 cup rice syrup (if you can't find rice syrup you may use
      honey or white sugar, but only 1/2 cup)
1 cup whole almonds
2–3 cups of unbleached flour (or whole wheat pastry flour)
1/2 teaspoon baking powder
1/2 cup carob powder

Optional ingredients: chocolate or carob chips, flaked coconut, raisins, dried apricot pieces, etc.

In a blender, grind the almonds as finely as possible. Cream together rice syrup and butter. Add vanilla and baking powder and mix. Add the almonds and mix again. Work in the flour (and carob powder) until you have a cookie-thickness dough. If the dough seems too dry, add vegetable oil by the teaspoonful to moisten it. Add the optional ingredients.

Take small hunks of the dough and roll into a ball. Place on greased cookie sheet and flatten with your hand or a fork. For New Moon cookies shape into crescents. Bake 10 minutes in a preheated 350 degree oven.

DARK MOON TEA

This tea blend will enhance your inner vision. Drink it at your Dark Moon ceremonies. (Never use metal pots or implements when brewing herbs; always use glass or earthen pots; additionally, use only pure, fresh water.)

Blend equal parts mugwort, bay leaves and rosebuds. Use 2 teaspoons per cup of boiling water. Cover and let steep 5 to 10 minutes.

FULL MOON TEA

Place 6–8 teaspoons of chickweed (ruled by the moon) in a quart glass jar (or use 4 teaspoons chickweed and 4 teaspoons of an herb ruled by the planetary ruler of sign of the zodiac within which the moon is full). Cover and set outside at moonrise on the night before the Full Moon. Let steep all night in the moonlight; bring in at sunrise, strain and refrigerate. The next night, the night of the Full Moon, drink it during your Full Moon ceremony.

GAELIC PRAYER TO THE NEW MOON
(from *Carmina Gadelica*)

Greetings to you, new moon, kindly jewel of guidance;
I bend my knees to you, I offer you my love.

I bend my knees to you, I raise my hands to you,
I lift my eyes to you, new moon of the seasons.

Greetings to you, new moon, darling of my love;
Greetings to you, new moon, darling of graces.

You journey on your course, you steer the flood tides;
You lift up your face for us, new moon of the seasons.

Queen of guidance, Queen of good luck,
Queen of my love, new moon of the seasons.

QUEEN OF THE NIGHT
(from *Carmina Gadelica*)

Hail unto thee,
Jewel of the night!

Beauty of the heavens,
Jewel of the night!

Mother of the stars,
Jewel of the night!

Fosterling of the sun,
Jewel of the night!

Majesty of the stars,
Jewel of the night!

A PRAYER TO THE MOON GODDESS
(author unknown)

Luna, every woman's friend,
To me thy goodness condescend,
Let me this night in visions see
Emblems of my destiny.

CHAPTER 14
PRAYERS

Prayer is a good way, in the hustle and bustle of our busy lives, to keep us connected to the Source. I am not speaking of prayer in the same sense that orthodox Christianity does with its emphasis on asking God for various "gifts" and "favors." Nor am I referring to it in the sense of constantly reminding ourselves how small and weak we are, and dependent on God's good mood. I use the word to mean, as stated above, connecting with Source, reminding ourselves of the greater reality of which we are a part. We can use prayer to tune in to the day's rhythms in much the same way as we use the Sabbats to tune into the year's rhythms and the moon tides to tune into the monthly rhythms. By this definition our Sabbat and Moon rituals are also prayers, but of a longer and more formal variety.

Morning prayers, night prayers and graces at mealtimes are helpful ways to do this "tuning in."

We can make our arising in the morning, going to bed at night and the eating of our meals rituals in their own right.

GRACES

Prayers said at mealtimes are referred to as graces. The purpose of graces said before meals is to bless and energize the food, to give thanks for the food (and the creatures, plant or animal, who gave their lives or energy that we might eat), and to be more consciously receptive of it. The purpose of graces said after meals is to give thanks for the food.

In our family, we rotate the job of selecting and starting the grace. Since there are six of us and seven days in a week there is a day for everyone and one left over (usually a parent takes this day). Sometimes we sing our graces. Through the years we have collected a few nice graces, sung and spoken. Here are some of them.

GRACES

1. Earth who gives us this food,
    Sun who makes it ripe and good,
    Dear Earth, Dear Sun, by you we live,
    Our loving thanks to you we give.
    (Christian Morgenstern)

2. We are thankful
    to the lives
    that give us this feast.
    (Marian Geraghty)

3. Blessings on the blossom,
    Blessings on the fruit,
    Blessings on the leaf and stem,
    Blessings on the root.

4. For health and strength and daily bread,
    We praise thy name, O Lord.
    For health and strength and daily bread,
    We praise thy name, O Lady.

5. For the golden corn,
    And the apples on the tree,
    For the golden butter,
    And the honey for our tea,
    For fruits and nuts and berries,
    That grow beside the way,
    or birds and beasts and flowers,
    We thank Thee everyday.

6. We thank the Water, Earth and Air
    And all the helping powers they bear—
    We thank the people—loving, good
    Who grow and cook our daily food.

And now at last we thank the Sun,
The light and life for everyone.

(origin unknown)

MORNINGS

MORNING PRAYER

As I rise up from my sleeping,
I give thanks for the night.
For sleep and dreams and resting
And for the morning's light.
Great Mother, Loving Father,
I thank thee for this day
And all is ahead of me,
Please guide me on my way.

EVENINGS

Evenings lend themselves well to night time rituals. Baths, bedtimes stories, cups of hot tea or cocoa, special prayers, story candles can all play a part. In our home it is easier to make the evenings into rituals than the mornings.

We find our kids usually require a prebedtime winding down period. When dinner is finished bath time begins. We always attempt to have bathtime be a tranquil time. Sometimes we try to make it special by having candles (no electric lights) and/or incense burning in the bathroom. We toss an herbal bath bag with sweet smelling herbs (easily made—see below) into the tub, and arrange 'grounding' stones (obsidian, hematite) around the edge. After bath, we help the kids into pajamas, read them a bedtime story and tuck them in with the following prayer. It adds a nice touch if you have a special candle that is lit at the beginning of the story and put out at the end of it. The above procedure works best with the under-nine set, though it can be adapted for older kids. Sometimes we do the story before bath, especially if we are reading a book that can be appreciated by all ages.

BATH BAG RECIPE

Make a small bag, about four inches by four inches, from muslin or cotton. Put the following herbs into the bag, then tie it tightly closed with a long piece of string or yarn. The string should be long enough so that the bag can hang from the faucet down into the tub to let the hot water run through it. The bath bag can be used for two successive nights.

3 tablespoons each of:

    Chamomile flowers
    Lavender flowers
    Rose petals
    Orange peel chunks

(1/2 cup oatmeal, ground in a blender, is optional. It is helpful for dry skin. The bag can be rubbed on the skin like a washcloth.)

Here is the prayer, written by our good friend JoAnn Adams for her children and happily adopted by us.

NIGHT PRAYER

As I go to sleep in bed,
Goddess linger near my head.
Keep me safely through the night
And greet me with the morning light.
Bless my friends and loved ones dear
Let me always feel them near.
Truth and beauty let me know,
Strength and honor let me grow.
Let nothing evil pass here,
Blessed be.

(Mark them with the sign of the pentagram while saying the last two lines.)

And from our friend Marian Geraghty, who was raising her children in the pagan way of life long before most of us were aware of the word, much less the concept, here is a beautiful night prayer.

Bright star that shines above
Bless and keep all those we love
Bless and keep us through the night
Till the morning star is bright
Blessed Be.

PART 3

Rites of Passage

INTRODUCTION

Among the valuable things we, as a culture, have lost, are our rites of passage. In other cultures rites of passage are clear cut markers as to where we are on the path of life. They make a statement to us, on inner and outer levels, as well as making a statement to the community in which we live, of where and who we are.

We have only a few of them left in our culture: weddings, funerals, baptisms, and baby showers being the most widely observed. But a baby shower doesn't make the same statement to our psyche as does a Blessingway ceremony (performed shortly before the birth of the baby), though one receives gifts for the new baby on both occasions.

The whole subject of men's rites of passage is only now beginning to be explored in the same way that women's rites of passage have been for the last several years. Lately, there has been an upsurge of interest in this subject and the formation of many men's groups. The men in these groups are working together to heal their wounds and define for themselves what it means to be a man, both in an individual and community context.

All major passages in our lives affect our community as well as our individual lives. This fact is not as obvious in this day and age as it was in previous ages. There are many new books coming out on this subject as it concerns both men and women; a listing of some of them will be found in the Suggested Reading section.

What follows is a brief explanation of, and examples of, various rites of passage. Here again, as in previous chapters, feel free to take the raw material offered herein and construct a ritual unique to your own situation. I'm hoping you will realize the importance of these rites, and work them into the rhythm of your lives.

CHAPTER 15

WOMEN'S MYSTERIES

The use of the word Blessingway comes from the Native American tradition, wherein such ceremonies are held to honor a person at various passages in his or her life. Many people these days are making use of the Blessingway format for women about to give birth and creating a new ritual from the old roots. Given below is the format and some ideas for creating one of your own.

In each Blessingway ceremony (indeed, in all rites of passage ceremonies) is the knowledge, whether stated or unstated, that one phase of life is ending and a new one is beginning. When a woman becomes a mother for the first time, the statement being made to the psyche by this event, and marked by the ceremony of the Blessingway, is that of leaving behind the maiden phase and entering the mother phase. When a woman becomes a mother for the second, third or even tenth time the statement made is that of the leaving behind of the previous status of mother of one, two or nine and expanding into the new phase of mothering, relating to and integrating within the existing family structure another being.

PREBIRTH BLESSINGWAY

The purpose of this ritual is to empower the expectant mother, to help her link with the Divine Mother as she prepares to pass through the most uniquely feminine of all the initiations—giving birth. This ritual should be done within two to three weeks of the due date.

Items needed for this ritual are:

small bottle of rosemary oil
clean hairbrush
large bowl
clean towel
cup of rose petals or rosebuds (can be either fresh or dried)
cup of lavender buds (fresh or dried)
large bowl containing two or three cups of cornmeal
very warm water in which to infuse the flowers
sage branch or smudge stick
small bowl or other container in which to place the smudge stick
ball of wool yarn
votive candle (optional)
pot of raspberry leaf (or other good pregnancy herb) tea
flower crown

At this ritual only women are allowed. They gather themselves into a circle, the expectant mother being seated in whatever way is the most comfortable to her. Every effort should be made to make her feel relaxed and venerated. In this ritual she is being recognized and honored as a channel of the Great Mother.

All sit in silent meditation for a few moments. The person leading the ritual says an opening prayer, invoking the powers of the four directions, the power of the One, and especially calling on the Great Mother. The prayer should contain a statement of the purpose of the ritual. After this a sage branch in a bowl or a smudge stick is passed around the circle and all smudge themselves.

A large bowl containing an infusion of rose petals and lavender buds is brought in. The water temperature should be warm, but not hot. Another large bowl containing about two or three cups of cornmeal is also brought in, as is a towel. One of the women is chosen to wash the mother's feet in the flower infusion. This is done in silence or accompanied by a song or chant as desired. The infusion bowl is removed and the mother's feet are then put into the bowl of cornmeal and massaged with the cornmeal. When this is finished they may be dusted off with the towel.

Another person is chosen to brush the mother's hair. She takes the bottle of rosemary oil, pours a tiny amount into her hand and massages it into the mother's hair. Then she brushes the hair, taking her time, playing with and pulling the hair gently to give as much pleasure as possible.

It is a nice touch to have ready a flower crown to place upon the mother's head after her hair has been brushed.

At this point raspberry tea is served to the mother, and others if they so desire.

A ball of wool yarn is brought into the circle and the leader winds it loosely around the mother's belly, measuring it. A knot is tied to mark the point. The yarn is passed from woman to woman around the circle, each speaking a blessing for the baby and mother, and tying a knot in it. When it comes around to the mother again, the leader takes it, breaks it off from the ball and gives it to the mother. Later this can be worn by the mother or made into a small item for the baby. (An alternative to this is for everyone to use a votive candle to make their wish. The candle is then set on the floor or altar.)

This may be followed by any birth or power chants known to the group.

An attempt can be made to psychically communicate with the baby, all sharing what they receive.

When this is finished, any gifts that have been brought may be given to the mother.

The circle may then be ritually closed, the powers of the directions thanked, and the Deities thanked. A feast or perhaps a small snack or dessert may then follow.

FIRST MOON

This ceremony is to honor a young girl at the time of her first moon blood. The occasion is of tremendous importance as it marks in a clear way the end of childhood and the beginning of womanhood. It is a physical transition—her body is now able to reproduce—but more development is needed in the mental and emotional realms before she can be considered an adult in every sense. A carefully thought out ritual at this time, as well as small private ones done every month at moon time, can aid in the transition and help her grow in her power as a woman.

This ritual can be very private, done by only the girl and her mother; very "women's mysteryish," done by or for the girl by her older female relatives and friends; or very public, done in a tribal/clan way in front of the whole of the pagan community with which the family is linked. The young woman's preference is definitely to be honored here. For an excellent and thorough treatment of this occasion (indeed, of all the Blood Mysteries), the book *Sister Moon Lodge* by Kisma Stepanich is highly recommended.

The ritual I have created for this occasion is somewhat loosely structured, to be used as a general framework and individualized for the person involved. The altar for this rite is a white cloth upon which a smaller red cloth has been placed. Place three altar candles, white, red and black, on it as well as a red and a white votive candle. Also on the altar should be a doll or other memento of childhood, any special power objects belonging to the girl, flowers, a token (stone or other talisman) representing the new stage of life being entered (you can see that this has to be extremely personal to the individual girl), and a ball of red wool yarn.

The oldest woman present shoul be designated Grandmother and will lead the ritual.

All lights are extinguished and all join hands and sit around the altar. The young girl is between the Grandmother and her own mother (if her own mother is not living or unable to be present, this role may be designated by the girl to someone else). The room should be as dark as possible. Time is spent in silence, centering.

GRANDMOTHER:
> From the darkness of the void Light is born.

The Mother lights the three altar candles.

MOTHER:
> White do we light for the Maiden,*
> Young one,
> Full of freshness, innocence and joy—
> We honor the time of childhood.
>
> Red do we light for the Mother,*
> Giver of life, beauty and abundance;
> Ripe, full of love and passion for many things.
> We honor the time of motherhood.
>
> Black do we light for the Crone,*
> Wise grandmother, who has seen many seasons
> Come and go;
> Old, wise, fierce
> We honor the time of cronehood.

GRANDMOTHER:
> Changing Woman,
> We love and honor you
> In all your changes.

A bowl of incense or sage is passed around and all smudge themselves.

GRANDMOTHER:
> We gather here to honor _____,
> As she passes from the Lodge of the Children
> To the Lodge of the Women.
> Let us call upon the Spirit Keepers
> For their aid and blessing.

EAST:
> Spirit Keepers of the East,
> Be with us today as we honor _____

As she passes into womanhood.
We ask that you share with us your gifts of knowledge and clear see-ing.

SOUTH:

Spirit Keepers of the South,
Be with us today as we honor _____
As she passes into womanhood.
We ask that you share with us your gifts of trust, of will, of far seeing.

WEST:

Spirit Keepers of the West,
Be with us today as we honor _____
As she passes into womanhood.
We ask that you share with us your gifts of compassion, fulfillment and inner seeing.

NORTH:

Spirit Keepers of the North,
Be with us today as we honor_____
As she passes into womanhood.
We ask that you share with us your gifts of patience, wisdom and deep seeing.

As each direction is invoked, the bowl of sage is lifted and offered in that direction.

GRANDMOTHER:

_____, you come among us today
As one newly passed into the lodge of the women,
A lodge that I, myself, have departed.
For as years pass the blood ceases to flow
At every moon, and then one enters
The Lodge of the Grandmothers.
We welcome you among us today;
And by our words, would now instruct you
In the meaning of this special passage.

The women present, beginning with the girl's mother and other relatives, now talk from their own experiences of what it means to be a woman, including the joys and responsibilities of sexuality, partnership and parenthood. Also the phases of the Moon and how its rhythms relate to women can be discussed. This should also include a wish or prayer for the young woman. Each woman, as she talks, holds the ball of yarn and unwinds a length of it. As she finishes her story she ties a knot in it and says:

Remember my words, and learn from them.

At the end of this part, the yarn is taken by one of the women and made into a necklace, bracelet or headband for the girl.

An alternative to the yarn would be for each woman to light a small candle as she tells her story and gives her wish. This could be concluded by the young woman herself speaking aloud her hopes and wishes for herself as a woman. The candles should be left to burn out.

Now follows a time of honoring the young woman. The older woman can give her a ritual bath (infusing the water with roses or other special herbs), or wash and massage her feet, brush her hair, adorn her in new clothes, jewelry, etc. (The intention here is to acknowledge her change of life status.) While this is being done, or at the conclusion, the following is to be spoken by the Grandmother.

GRANDMOTHER:
> The way of woman is the way of the shaman.
> For truly, the act of giving birth
> Is the ultimate shamanic journey,
> As we bring a being from the world of spirit
> Into the world of matter.
>
> All humans are creative beings,
> Able to tap into the realms of spirit for inspiration.
> But women have been gifted with their moontime,
> A time of natural inward journeying,
> To make this easier.
>
> Women are—body, mind and spirit—
> Walkers between the worlds.
> When the blood flows from you each month,
> Be aware that the journey becomes easier,
> As the veils between the worlds thin and dissolve.
>
> Allow yourself the time and silence to
> Journey to the spirit realms each month,
> To dream your dreams, to see your visions,
> And bring back with you
> The gifts and wisdom of the ancestors,
> For yourself, for your family, for your clan.
> And someday, by mutual choosing, one of the ancestors
> May return again, through your womb.

MOTHER:
> Let us thank the Spirit Keepers

For their presence.

EAST:

> Spirit Keeper of the East,
> We thank you for your presence among us,
> And the gifts you bring.
> Hail and farewell!

SOUTH:

> Spirit Keeper of the South,
> We thank you for your presence among us,
> And the gifts you bring.
> Hail and farewell!

WEST:

> Spirit Keeper of the West,
> We thank you for your presence among us,
> And the gifts you bring.
> Hail and farewell!

NORTH:

> Spirit Keeper of the North,
> We thank you for your presence among us,
> And the gifts you bring.
> Hail and farewell.

MOTHER:

> Great Mother, we thank you
> For the gifts of life, love,
> And the special woman-gift
> Of being a channel for the creative force
> In its many forms.
> Blessed Be!

The rite is concluded by a feast including the young woman's favorite foods.

If it is wished to include the male members of the family, they can be allowed to prepare and serve the feast.

---

* These lines were written by Ed Fitch and are used here with his permission.

CHAPTER 16

MEN'S MYSTERIES

I have to admit that this section of the book was the most difficult for me to write. Meaningful rites of passage for men in our society have been almost nonexistent. What has our culture been able to offer our male children as they pass into manhood? Team sports, the college entrance exams, beer parties and overemphasis on casual sex spring to mind. And of course the draft, which, when it is in effect, forces our young men to steel themselves against their feelings about losing their lives just as they reach their full physical flowering. What kind of societal support or preparation does a man receive when embarking upon marriage or fatherhood, or indeed, adult life?

It is my feeling that positive, life-affirming male rituals are desperately needed in our society. Rituals wherein young men can learn to honor their roles as protector, as manifester; rituals wherein men can learn to value their strength, the beauty of their bodies, their dreams and visions; rituals wherein the older men offer guidance from their own experience to those about to marry or become fathers, or embark upon any other uniquely male experience.

Happily, these rituals are beginning to manifest in some communities. Men are coming together, talking, creating ritual and gaining much in the process. And as they do so, the concepts of what it is to be a man, as well as their concept of the male aspect of the Divine, are examined, deepened and redefined.

In writing this chapter I have consulted with men who are leading or belonging to some of the local men's groups. I have found that men in these groups are deeply involved in a process of redefining, trying to understand their masculinity.

There have been charges leveled by some women's groups that men's groups tend to indulge in "women bashing." I have found that, to a certain extent, this can be true, but it is only part of the picture.

The men's movement seems to be moving through stages, just as the women's movement did (and still does), of what I can only describe as "defining of self by reaction to the other." Men's rituals seem to be more focused on "separation from" in order to grow to the next phase, whereas women's rituals seem to emphasize more the elements of "stepping into" or "embracing the wholeness" with regards to phases of life. Nowhere do I see anything but the embryonic beginnings of an acknowledgment of the dance men and women must do together, if life on this planet is to survive.

I find that I am in deep disagreement with the major thrust of the "separation from" aspect of the men's movement. This particular aspect seems to feel a need to break away, sharply and abruptly, to sever its connection with the feminine principle (as represented by the women in their life) in order to find their masculinity. Similarly, some factions of the women's movement seem to have felt a need to sever connection with the Male Principle (as represented by the men in their life) to find their true feminine nature.

I realize that the purpose here is "separation as an aid to self definition." But while it is, indeed, a good thing to claim one's own power and deal with what feels oppressive, it is important to realize that men can never be truly separate from women, just as women can never be truly separate from men because *we all contain that other half within ourselves.* We are bipolar beings, physically manifesting one gender, but containing both within us. All of us have a feminine dimension and a masculine dimension and both are necessary and sacred parts of our wholeness. And both demand *true* expression, not the distorted stereotypical nonsense we've been fed from the prevailing culture, not to mention the fact that because both genders inhabit the planet together it is imperative that we recognize that we are interwoven.

When I look at the whole arena of the women's/men's movements, what I see is an outward manifestation of an inner struggle. What is the inner struggle really about? It is the struggle to identify oneself as a unique and whole individual in a world of seeming dualities. Male, female, light, dark, inward, outward—we are surrounded by dualities that seem to be suggesting that we make choices between them, instead of seeing them as opposites sides of the same coin of our wholeness.

The problems arise when we take our outwardly manifesting gender to be the totality of who we are. If we identify ourselves as "man" or "woman" exclusively then it would seem that we are *not* "the other" in any way. The danger here is that the "other" might possibly be seen to be so completely separate from us as to be a probable cause of whatever we perceive as wrong. Carried to extremes this separation becomes one that happens within us and instead of being helpful in our self definition, only serves to further fragment us. (I might add that one could write "gay" or "straight" into this equation and the answer would be the same. I might further add that this happens on a collective, societal level as well as a personal one.)

Men searching their souls and psyches in a deep and truthful manner for definition of masculinity will inevitably come into interaction with the feminine principle we call the Goddess, just as women will come upon the God, the masculine principle, in the course of their inner work.

It is my hope that the men's movement, as it goes through its stages, does not make the same mistakes that I perceive the the women's movement to have made, and occasionally continues to make: The rejection of one aspect (i.e. masculine principle *or* feminine principle) for the supposed gain of the other.

We are all here in service to the greater wholeness that is All Life, not just to do our own personal lives. We are all in relationship to each other, as well as to the earth and all life forms. To bond with the feminine side of our nature allows us to see and feel this. To bond with the masculine side of our nature allows us to take action to manifest this. Both sides of ourselves are necessary if we are to truly be the creative beings life means us to be.

Since this ritual process for men is still in its beginning stages, I can offer you only guidelines for creating these rituals in your own life, in your own way.

MANHOOD COMING OF AGE RITUAL

This ritual marks the transition from boyhood into young manhood. It should be done sometime around the onset of puberty. This will very somewhat from person to person, but generally is between the ages of 12–14.

The young person is leaving childhood and entering the lodge of the men. His relationships with parents and friends subtly, but definitely, alter as those around him acknowledge that he can no longer be treated as a child, but is not quite yet a fully grown and responsible adult. His body changes, he takes on new responsibilities with the context of family and society. He is in training with his male elders for his lifelong job of being a mature, responsible member of his society. It is very important at this age to provide good role modeling as well as mentors for the adolescent. Teenagers are not quite the avid imitators that younger children are, but it is still a factor. They observe, they question, they rebel. During this process they need firm ground to stand upon, and something solid to push against as they learn about themselves and their world. A ritual marking this time as a specific milepost on their journey through life would be of definite benefit to them.

This ritual is one that can be used to mark this passage.

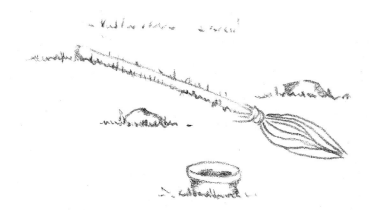

YOUNG MANHOOD RITUAL

This ritual should be done, if at all possible, outdoors, in a remote, private area. If this is not possible, a fenced backyard will suffice. Failing all the above, indoors will do.

In attendance at this ritual are the boy's father, the adult male members of the community, and the boy's grandfather. If the boy's father is unable to be present, this role may be designated by the boy to someone else. If the grandfather is unable to be present, then the oldest man present shall be designated as Grandfather.

The ritual area is set up within a Medicine Wheel-type stone circle which has been designed within the context of one of the following four patterns:

1) 12 stones for the 12 months of the year

2) 13 stones for the 13 moons of the year

3) 4 stones for the 4 seasons of the year and the 4 directions

4) 8 stones for the 8 directions of E, SE, S, SW, W, NW, N, NE, and the 8 Sabbats.

The individual stones are brought by the men who will be in attendance; and at the beginning of the rite the stone should be placed appropriately and with intention. Within the stone circle should be easy-to-use body paints, as well as representations of the four elements: a container of water, a container of earth or cornmeal, a smudge stick or sage branch to represent the air element, and fire in the form of a bonfire, torch, and/or candles. Also needed is a bundle containing "Man clothing" with which to clothe the young man at the conclusion of the rite. This clothing can be anything the father and other male elders decide is appropriate and symbolic. A drum is useful but not necessary.

To begin the ritual, the men enter the area and set the stones around, according to the chosen pattern and with the intention of activating that particular energy.

Mother brings the boy to the outside edge of the stone circle.

MOTHER *(while removing his clothing):*
>   Naked you were
>   When born from my body,
>   And naked you must be
>   As you go forth from me now.

She turns to the boy's father.

>   He is ready to enter the lodge of the men.
>   With love, and the blessings of the Mother,
>   I give him into your keeping.

She blindfolds the boy, kisses him and leaves. Father comes forth, followed by a group of the adult men of the community. The men form a circle around the boy and Father and Grandfather. Father and Grandfather pick up the container of earth or cornmeal (or alternatively, handfuls of earth from the ground beneath them) and pour them over his feet, then his head.

FATHER & GRANDFATHER:
>   Remember your Mother, the Earth.

They lift and turn his head till he is looking skyward.

>   Remember your Father, the Sky.

The four men chosen to guard the directions assume their places by the stones in each direction. Father and Grandfather lead the boy to the eastern quarter, and present him.

>   Spirit Keepers of the East,
>   Place of dawn, of childhood, of new beginnings, of life;
>   We ask you to be with us
>   And to witness that_____
>   Is now ready to begin the process of becoming a man.

The man standing in the East smudges him with sage and a feather.

EAST:

> By the power of eagle
> May you learn to fly high and see far.

He hands the boy the feather, and Father, Grandfather and the boy move on to the South.

FATHER & GRANDFATHER:

> Spirit Keepers of the South,
> Place of noon, of youth, of growth, of light;
> We ask you to be with us and to witness that_____
> Is now ready to begin the process of becoming a man.

The man standing in the South is holding a candle or a torch. He circles the boy with the torch/candle.

SOUTH:

> By the power of mouse, may you learn to trust.
> By the power of coyote, may you learn to laugh at yourself.
> With trust and laughter, may you move into the light of growth.

He hands the boy the torch/candle and Father, Grandfather and the boy move on to the West.

FATHER & GRANDFATHER:

> Spirit Keepers of the West,
> Place of twilight, of maturity, of love;
> We ask you to be with us and to witness that_____
> Is now ready to begin the process of becoming a man.

The man in the West is holding an earthen vessel containing water. He sprinkles it on the boy.

WEST:

> By the power of bear
> May you learn to harvest and digest
> The fruits of your experiences,
> And let go of that which no longer serves you.

He hands the boy the vessel, and Father, Grandfather (who can help carry these objects if desired) and the boy move on to the North.

FATHER AND GRANDFATHER:

> Spirit Keepers of the North,
> Place of midnight, of age and death, of law;
> We ask you to be with us and to witness that_____
> Is now ready to begin the process of becoming a man.

The man in the North is holding a clear or white quartz crystal. Beginning at the boy's feet he moves it upward in a straight line, ending by touching the boy's sixth and seventh chakras (forehead and top of head) with it, saying:

NORTH:
> By the power of buffalo may you learn wisdom.
> By the power of crystal may you become clear in your essence.

He hands the boy the crystal.

The gifts of the four directions are taken from the boy and put on the ground in the center of the circle. The men representing the other four directions/months/moons now take their places at each of the stones, forming a circle around the boy, Father and Grandfather. Any other men form an outer circle. The boy, still blindfolded, is now led around the circle. He stops in front of each man, who speaks to him, from the heart, about the particular phase of life represented by each of the positions/directions/seasons/moons around the wheel of life. Obviously, the man chosen to represent each station should be able to speak knowledgeably and from experience. When he is finished speaking the man twirls the boy around three times and pushes him over to the next man. The purpose of the twirling and pushing is to make the boy dizzy and disoriented. His job is then to remain on his feet throughout. Drumming matching the boy's energy can be happening now if a drum and drummer are present.

When the boy comes around again to the East, he is stopped suddenly and the blindfold is removed. The circle closes in tighter around him and the men offer their congratulations to him for his endurance.

They then take up the body paints and paint his body with male symbols (solar, phallic, Green Man, etc.) and then, if desired, paint themselves. When this is done, the boy is then dressed in the "man clothing" and given gifts symbolic of his new status. These gifts can be objects to help him "live out" the powers of the four directions. Some suggestions are:

AIR — books, knives, bow and arrow, mental objects
FIRE — art materials, pens and journals, a piece of wood to make into a staff, self expression objects
WATER — meditation tape, dream journal, intuitive, introspective objects
EARTH — drum, medicine shield and/or pouch makings, grounding objects

After the presentation of the gifts, refreshments (prepared by the women of the family) are brought forth and enjoyed by all.

When it is time to end the ceremony, the man at each of the four directions (beginning in the East), gives thanks to the spirits in the following manner:

SPEAKER:

> Spirit Keepers of the _____,
> We thank you for your gifts to us,
> And to this boy-become-a-man.
> Farewell and blessed be!

This is repeated at each of the other directions.

Standing in the center of the circle, the boy prays a spontaneous prayer of thanksgiving to the All Father for his life and his community.

Lifting their hands over his head, the Father and Grandfather say:

FATHER & GRANDFATHER:

> Divine Spirit that manifests in many forms,
> We give you thanks for this young man.
> We ask your assistance,
> That we may guide him well on his path.
> We thank you also for this day, this life, these friends.
> May we always recognize our brotherhood with each other,
> And know that we are all children of the same divine parents.
> Blessed be!

THE FATHERHOOD INITIATION

This ceremony occurs when a man is about to become a father for the first time. Ideally, it should be done at the same time his wife is undergoing the Blessingway ceremony.

The ritual area should be set up with an altar in the center. On the altar place a cauldron and in it a wand decorated with ribbons. A circle of votive candles should surround the cauldron. A cup or drinking horn and a bowl containing smudging materials should be nearby. Place a flask of hot herbal tea (mugwort and bay is a good mixture for this occasion) on or under the altar. A staff encircled with greenery should be leaning against the altar, or available nearby.

All men present at this ceremony should be fathers.

Four men assume the positions as Guardians of the directions. The other men group themselves as follows:

In the East, those having something to share concerning the new father's role in the prenatal period as well as his role of keeping the focus in the actual birthing process.

In the South, those having something to share concerning his role as new father, assisting with the day to day tasks, learning to be a protector and defender in the sense of taking care of the new mother-child-father unit so the necessary growth/bonding can occur. Also those who can share with him their wisdom and experience about young, growing children (the fun of fatherhood).

In the West, those having something to share with regards to reminding him to remember and care for his own needs well enough so that he can continue functioning. Also those who can share with him their wisdom and experience dealing with older children and their specific needs (when to hold on, when to let go).

In the North, those having something to share concerning the deep wisdoms and hard won lessons of fatherhood, as well as the deep responsibilities thereof (offering just enough guidance to the older child to allow him/her to make their own "learning" mistakes).

Throughout, both the fun and serious aspects of fatherhood should be stressed.

When all are gathered and in their places, there is a moment of silent meditation and grounding, then the Sentinels of the Four Directions speak, beginning with the South.

SOUTH:
> In passion it begins.

NORTH:
> In wisdom it ends.

WEST:
> Along the way true love is learned.

EAST:
> And awareness grows.

SOUTH:
> Spirits of the South, we ask for heartfulness.

NORTH:
> Spirits of the North, we ask for endurance, and patience.

WEST:
> Spirits of the West, we ask for spiritual nourishment.

EAST:
> Spirits of the East, we ask for discernment.

PRIEST:
> May the circle of our love bind us all together.

A smudge stick or sage branch is passed around, each person smudging the person next to him.

The Priest takes up the staff and pounds it on the ground three times.

PRIEST:
> Hear now the wisdom
> Of those who have traveled this path before you.
> Listen well, that you may learn.

Now the men present, beginning in the East, share their experiences relative to that direction, and tell about what being a father means to them and how it has changed their lives. As each man speaks, he hold the staff, which is used as a talking stick and is passed to the next person in due course. The new father is encouraged to interact and ask questions.

The Priest now pours the tea into the cup/horn and passes it around the circle for each man to sip from, refilling it as necessary until all the tea in the flask has been consumed.

After this, all are encouraged to visualize the mother and tune into the spirit of the baby. Then the Priest begins drumming a heartbeat rhythm and creating a spirit song that will help the baby's spirit find its right time and place to be born, and to aid it in making the transition from the spirit world to the physical world. When it feels appropriate, refreshments can be served.

When it is time to finish, the new father gives thanks in his own words for the gift of fatherhood, and for the love and counsel of his elders (brothers, father and grandfathers).

PRIEST:

We give thanks for the wisdom shared this day,
We give thanks for the spirit helpers who have guided us,
Who continue to help and guide us,
As we walk this good walk, and live this good life upon the earth.
Let us be ever mindful of the brotherhood we share,
One with another.
Let us be ever mindful of the love that binds us together,
Men, women, four-leggeds, two-leggeds, finned ones, feathered ones.
Sun, moon and stars in the sky, earth beneath our feet.
May we walk in balance.

CHAPTER 17

YOUTH PASSAGES

BIRTH

The birth of a child into the family/community is cause for celebration and rejoicing. All the many aspects of this event can be handled in a sacred way.

The birth itself is such a holy event that every attempt should be made to carry it out in a meaningful way. Whether it takes place in a hospital, birth center, or at home, the event can be ritualized, a circle cast, the Spirit Keepers summoned and the Deities invoked. There are special spirits (some call them angels) that are present at each and every birth. The act of tuning into them and tuning into the powerful energy around birth creates a ritual in and of itself.

Much attention should be given to assisting the laboring woman in whatever way she needs. Some women wish privacy, some not; some desire massage, labor coaching, encouragement. There are herbs to facilitate the process. These are best handled by one well-versed in herbalism, but raspberry leaf tea, warm, cold or frozen into ice chips, is a safe and welcome respite at any time during the labor process. This I can personally vouch for!

After the birth has occurred a special meal is in order, for the mother will no doubt be ravenously hungry after such a large energy expenditure. The father, if he has helped and supported the mother throughout labor and birth, will undoubtedly be more tired than hungry, since he has not had the hormonal support nature has provided for the birthing mother. But surely both mother and father will want to celebrate the special event, and a special meal, thoughtfully provided by members of the community, is a practical form of celebration.

To party or not to party after a home birth is always an individual decision, but personal experience has led me to the conclusion that the best way is to share the joy (in a quiet way) with immediate family or close friends and to always carefully watch the mother's energy level. Bear in mind also that the child is new to this plane of existence and should be allowed to get use to noise and high energy levels in a gradual way.

THE CEREMONY OF SAINING

The word "sain" comes from the Old English "segnian" which means "to mark with a sign." Athough saining originally had to do with a purification by fire ritual, the word eventually came to mean "bless." A Saining is a traditional European child naming and blessing ceremony that takes place shortly after the birth of the child, within the first nine days of the child's life. It is said to involve trees; perhaps the child was taken outdoors to an area sacred to the family or clan and introduced to the guardian spirits of the area residing within certain trees. Or perhaps a tree was planted to give thanks for the birth. The tree, at any rate, stands as witness to the naming of the child. The name chosen for the child is first revealed at this ceremony, spoken aloud for the first time by the mother if the child is a girl, or by the father if the child is a boy. The child is introduced to the friends and family in attendance and to the four directions by this name. Gifts may be given to the child, either material gifts or spiritual gifts in the form of good wishes. Sometimes the placenta and/or umbilical cord are buried at the foot of the tree as both an offering and as a link between the child and the tree. As usual in pagan ceremonies, a goodly feast is appropriate to conclude the ceremonies.

The following is an example of a modern day Saining ceremony.

In this modern age most of us are not living in areas where large, wild, forested, sacred sites are easily accessible. Therefore, adapt this ceremony as your need dictates. What IS required is a bit of land (your backyard, a city park, etc.) that has growing on it a tree that feels special and powerful to you. Ideally, a search for this area should begin before the baby is born.

Once the site has been chosen, the parents should visit it as frequently as possible and spend much time tuning in to the nature spirits of the area. The parents should inform the spirits of their intention and open themselves psychically to determine if assent is given.

When the time for the ceremony has arrived those gathered should form themselves into a procession, led by those designated as Priest and Priestess of the ceremony. The parents and child come next, followed by the family and then by the guests. The Priestess should carry a wooden staff, the Priest a large cup or other vessel containing water. Whichever parent is not carrying the baby will carry the vessel containing the placenta or umbilicus.

One of the guests will carry a small shovel or garden trowel.

When the tree is reached all proceed around it three times and form themselves into a circle. The parents, priest and priestess step into the center of the circle and it closes behind them. The implements are placed upon the ground and the staff is set against the tree.

PRIEST:

> We gather here today for the saining of this new, small one.
> For all children born must have a name,
> And the naming of a child is a grave matter,
> Worthy of serious consideration.
> Names have power and virtue,
> Names can bind and limit.
> Names are carried throughout life,
> And never fail to affect the bearer.
>
> Have you thought deeply on this matter
> And chosen an appropriate name
> For the spirit entrusted to your care?

PARENTS:

> Yes, we have.

PRIEST:

> Then let the saining begin!

Priestess casts the circle (going around the tree so that it is included in the circle) using the staff.

PRIESTESS:

> I carve out the boundaries of our sacred circle,
> And I weave into being around us a circle of radiant light;
> Guarding us, protecting us,
> Allowing in only that which is of service.
> In the names of the Great Mother and Father of us all.

She goes to each of the four directions in turn and summons:

> Great Guardians of the_____,
> We request your presence here today
> At this ceremony of saining.
> Come! And be welcome among us!

She walks the boundaries of the circle and invokes:

> Nature spirits, devas,
> We recognize your presence here among us!
> You are welcome at this ceremony of saining!

She returns to the center of the circle.

> Great Mother of all,
> Mighty Father,
> First manifestations of the great mystery,
> Without you we would not be.
> We honor you.
> Accept our thanks and love
> For the blessing of the new one who has come among us.

PRIEST:
> Let the child now be brought forth!

The parents step forward with the child.

PRIESTESS:
> Here now, as in ancient times,
> Shall this child be named and blessed.
> Stand here, against this tree,
> Sacred guardian of the land,
> And feel the life-force flowing through it,
> Just as it flows through us all.
>
> Touch your child to this tree,
> And feel the forces combine, mingle:
> Yours, the child's, the tree's—
> And know the oneness of life.

There is a short pause while this takes place. She continues:

> By the witness of this tree,
> Sacred guardian of this land,
> What name have you chosen for this child?

The parents respond, giving the name, and if desired, their reasons for choosing it.

The Priestess repeats the name aloud and begins singing it, chanting it. The chant is taken up by those present and the singing should reflect their love for the child.

PRIESTESS:
> Henceforth, small one,
> By the name_____ shall you be known.

The person with the shovel comes forward and digs a hole large enough to hold the placenta/umbilical cord (deep enough to discourage wandering dogs). One of the parents buries these in the hole.

PARENT:

Let these ever link you
To the trees and to the land, little one.
That you may be known by them
For as long as your life shall endure.

The Priestess hands the bowl of water to the parents and they pour it onto the site. The Priest comes forward and guides the parents (holding the baby) to the Eastern quarter, and then to each of the subsequent quarters.

PRIEST:

Mighty Ones of the _____,
This is_____,
Child of the Goddess and God,
Newly come among us.

PRIESTESS:

Let all present now offer their gifts and good wishes.

One by one those present come forward and offer their gifts, physical and spiritual. (The spiritual gifts can be as simple as "I wish for this child the gift of balance," or beauty, or kindness, or wisdom, etc. The physical gifts can be stones, feathers, seashells, or symbols or tokens of the spiritual gifts.)

PRIEST:

The child has been named and made known.
The saining is complete.
Let us thank the Mighty Ones who have graced us with their presence.

The Priestess goes around to each of the four directions.

PRIESTESS:

Guardian Spirits of the _____
We do thank you for your presence
And now bid you farewell.

She walks the boundary of the circle.

Nature spirits and devas,
We thank you for welcoming us among you.
Blessed be!

She comes back to the center of the circle.

Great Mother of us all,
Mighty Father of us all,
We thank you for life, for love, for laughter,

And especially for this new small being
Who has come among us!
Blessed be!
This rite is ended, merry meet and merry part.

ALL:
And merry meet again.

* * * * * * * * * * * * * * * * * * * *

Another rite of passage is that of the young one being introduced and dedicated to the Deities of the parents/clan. The following ceremony can be used for this purpose.

RITE OF DEDICATION FOR A SMALL CHILD

This rite should be performed as the Moon is waxing, and preferably near to an appropriate seasonal festival.

This ritual is designed to be somewhat tribal in nature. It is written to be performed by Priest, Priestess, Guardians of the Directions, Parents, and Godparents. The lines can be apportioned out (when appropriate) to those present to give the feel of community involvement. I envision it as a ceremony performed by the elders of the tribe/clan to ceremonially bring the child to the attention of, as well as dedicate the child to, the clan's Deities.

Needed for this ritual are a large piece of cloth to serve as an altar cloth, a bell, a chalice, a bowl of earth, incense, two altar candles, a votive candle, a ceremonial broom, a staff, nine or thirteen stones/crystals (to represent the eight Sabbats and the center point, or the thirteen moons of the year).

If performed outside, all should march in procession to the ritual area. After all have gathered there should be a few moments of silence while all focus on the intention of the ritual.

The Priestess sweeps the circle area with her broom, sets up the altar with a cloth, chalice, bowl of earth, incense, two altar candles and a votive candle, all of which have been carried to the area in a basket. Guests should assist by placing stones and crystals around the circumference of the circle (eight or twelve), using the largest ones at the four quarters. The Priestess puts the ninth (or thirteenth) stone on the altar. When all is in readiness and all are standing in a circle (and the Sentinels of each direction are at their station), the Priestess, who is facing North, speaks.

PRIESTESS:
We gather here now

To dedicate this small one to the Old Gods.
That his/her life may be full and satisfying,
And in harmony with the forces of nature,
That he/she shall achieve his/her full potential in life,
That he/she may always be surrounded
By the love and the protection of the Old Gods.

The elements are silently consecrated. Then the Priestess, followed by the Priest carrying the staff, casts the circle, by walking the circumference.

PRIEST & PRIESTESS:
We weave into being around us
A circle of radiant light;
Guarding us, protecting us,
Allowing in only that which is good and true,
And of service,
In the names of the great Mother and Father of us all.

This is done three times.

The Priestess blesses the person to her left with the consecrated water and smudges them, and they do likewise to the person on their left, all the way around the circle.

PRIESTESS:
Let the Guardian Spirits now be summoned!

The Sentinel of the East begins.

EAST:
Guardian Spirits of the East,
You who bring the brilliance of dawn,
The freshness of spring;
You who bring new beginnings to our lives;
We call upon you to be with us now,
To give your blessings to this child,
And ever look favorably on him/her.
You are welcome here among us!
Blessed be!

SOUTH:
Guardian Spirits of the South,
You who bring the brilliant clarity of midday,
The warmth, growth and strength of summer;
You who bring the fire of idealism to our lives;
We call upon you to be with us now,
To give your blessings to this child,

And ever look favorably on him/her.
You are welcome here among us!
Blessed be!

WEST:

Guardian Spirits of the West,
You who bring the deep shadows of the sunset,
You who guard the place of dreams and healing;
You who bring balance and introspection to our lives;
We call upon you to be with us now,
To give your blessings to this child,
And ever look favorably on him/her.
You are welcome among us!
Blessed be!

NORTH:

Guardian Spirits of the North,
You who bring the restful stillness of winter,
You who bring patience, practicality,
Wisdom and ritual to our lives;
We call upon you to be with us now,
To give your blessings to this child,
And ever look favorably on him/her.
You are welcome among us!
Blessed be!

PRIESTESS:

Nature spirits, devas!
We recognize your presence here among us!
Accept our greetings and love, you are welcome among us!
Blessed be!

PRIEST *(holding aloft staff)*:

Wise and loving All-Father,
Friend and helper of all living creatures;
We ask that you be here among us now.
We ask that you strengthen and protect
This child who shall be dedicated to the Old Ways.
We bid you welcome!

PRIESTESS *(holding aloft chalice)*:

O most Ancient One—
We call upon you by your many titles:
Star Mother, Earth Mother, Great Mother, Grandmother—
We ask that you be here among us now.

We ask that in your all-encompassing mother-love
You will give shelter, protection and guidance
To this small and sacred child
Who shall be dedicated to the Old Ways.
We bid you welcome!

A bell is sounded five times.

PRIEST:
Let the child be brought forth

The parents, holding the child, now step forward and stand before the altar.

PRIESTESS:
Who is it that comes before the Old Gods,
To be dedicated to their service
And placed under their protection?

PARENTS:
It is _____, one newly come to this world.

PRIESTESS:
And who is it that speaks for him/her?

PARENTS:
I, _____, and I, _____, parents of this small one.

PRIESTESS:
And what is it you have to say,
Before those gathered here, and in the presence of the Gods?

PARENTS:
We are here to present this child
And dedicate him/her to the Old Ones.
Before our friends, before our families,
Before our ancestors, especially those who have followed the Old
Ways,
Before the guardian spirits of the four directions,
Before the guardian spirits of this land, before the Old Gods;
Our child being too young to speak for him/herself,
We do speak for him/her,
Till he/she is old enough to speak his/her own will.

Priestess picks up the plate of earth.

PRIESTESS:
For one of this young and gentle age
A purification is not truly needed.

Yet let now his/her hand touch this earth
Here before us.

The child's hand is touched to the earth on the plate. Priestess touches him/her.

PRIESTESS:
To Earth art thou made known, O small one.

Priestess picks up the censer of incense.

PRIESTESS:
Let now his/her hand touch this sweet air here before us.

The child's hand is passed through the smoke of the incense. Priestess touches him/her.

PRIESTESS:
To Air art thou made known, O small one.

Priestess picks up candle.

PRIESTESS:
Let now his/her hand feel the warmth of this fire here before us.

The child's hand is passed above the candle. Priestess touches him/her.

PRIESTESS:
To Fire art thou made known, O small one.

Priestess picks up the chalice of water.

PRIESTESS:
Let now his/her hand touch this water here before us.

Child's fingers are dipped into the water.

PRIESTESS:
To Water art thou made known, O small one.

Priestess continues while blessing the child with both hands.

By Earth, by Air, by Fire, by Water,
Small and holy one,
Art thou purified and made known.

The father takes the child. The Priest comes forth, holds his hands over the child in an attitude of blessing.

PRIEST:
May the blessings of the All-Father,
Strong, wise and protective,
Be upon you, little one!

May you grow strong and skillful under His protection,
And be a true friend to all living beings.

The mother takes the child. Priestess comes forth, holds her hands over the child in an attitude of blessing.

PRIESTESS:

May the blessings of the Triple Goddess,
Of Maiden, of Mother, of Crone,
Beautiful, loving and wise,
Be upon you, little one!
May you grow strong and wise under Her protection,
And always seek for truth.

A bell is sounded three times and there is a pause.

PRIEST:

You who would dedicate this child to the Old Ways,
I bid you both to put your hands on this sacred altar,
And listen well to what we say.
For the pledge you are about to take is a most serious one,
And not a matter to be lightly undertaken.

PRIESTESS:

I bid you both to give your child
A calm, warm and loving home.
Let peace prevail between you
That your child feel secure and loved.
Raise your child with gentleness
And surrounded by beauty.

PRIEST:

I bid you both to teach well
The soul that has been entrusted to you,
Giving your child a good foundation
In matters of manners, and respect for others.
Offer also to your child the best you can in matters academic,
That he/she may be ready to take his/her rightful place
Among his/her peers when grown.

PRIESTESS:

I bid you both to give your child
Respect for his/her own unique individuality.
I bid you, by your example, to teach your child,
A sense of awe and wonder toward the world of nature,
A sense of joy for the gift of life,

And a sense of responsibility
Toward the other living beings on the planet,
And indeed, toward our Mother, the earth, Herself.

PRIESTESS & PRIESTESS:
Have you listened and understood our counsel?

PARENTS:
We have.

PRIESTESS:
If you are ready to assume these duties
As parents of this small and sacred child,
Take now your vows before the gods.

PARENTS:
We,_____ and _____,
As pagan parents,
Do take these sacred vows,
Before the Goddess and before the God:

We promise to provide a safe and happy home.
We promise to love our child unconditionally,
To respect his/her god(dess)hood,
And to teach well the Old Religion and live as we teach;
But to remember that he/she is on his/her own path,
And we are here to help him/her find the way.
We promise to remember that
No matter how young the body may be,
The soul is not young.

We also promise to be aware
That he/she has as much to teach us
As we have to teach him/her.
And finally, we promise that he/she shall learn
That the earth is his/her Mother
And he/she is kin to all creatures.

These things, for our child and ourselves, do we vow.
So be it.

The bell is rung three times; Priestess raps with the staff.

PRIESTESS:
If there are those present who would stand as godparents
To this little one,
Let them now come forth and stand before this sacred altar.

Godparents encircle the parents, child and altar.

PRIESTESS:

    Are you now ready to assume the duties of godparents?
    Are you willing to love and guide the child
    As if he/she were of your own blood,
    To teach the young one, by word and example,
    That he/she may learn the Craft of the Wise
    And grow strong in our ancient wisdoms?
    Are you now ready to assume these responsibilities?

GODPARENTS:

    We are ready to assume these responsibilities.

PRIESTESS:

    Place your hands on this sacred altar
    As you swear to take on this task.

Godparents place their hands on the altar.

GODPARENTS:

    In the name of the All-Father,
    In the name of the Great Mother of all,
    Do we take upon ourselves the grave responsibility
    As godparents of _____.

At this point they come forward one by one and each state personally their intentions as godparents. A small gift of a natural object such as a stone, feather, shell, etc. can be given in token of this. The gifts are placed on a tray on the altar. In conclusion, all present gather around the tray, extend their hands over the gifts and bless them silently.

GODPARENTS:

    These gifts, small and dear one, do we give to you,
    That your body, mind and soul
    May strengthen and grow, enriching the world in all ways;
    And drawing you to be one with the forces and beings of nature.

When this is concluded, all go back to their original places in the circle. Then the child is carried around by the parents and presented in turn to each of the four directions, as the sentinel of that directions speaks.

EAST:

    Guardian Spirits of the East,
    Witness now that _____ is dedicated to the old ways.
    We give you our thanks!
    Hail and farewell!

Candle is extinguished.

SOUTH:
>Guardian Spirits of the South,
>Witness now that _____ is dedicated to the old ways.
>We give you our thanks!
>Hail and farewell!
>*Candle is extinguished.*

WEST:
>Guardian Spirits of the West,
>Witness now that _____ is dedicated to the old ways.
>We give you our thanks!
>Hail and farewell!
>*Candle is extinguished.*

NORTH:
>Guardian Spirits of the North,
>Witness now that _____ is dedicated to the old ways.
>We give you our thanks!
>Hail and farewell!
>*Candle is extinguished.*

The child is lifted up in the direction of the sky.

PRIEST:
>Ancient and wise All-Father,
>Witness, now, we do ask, that _____
>Has by this rite been dedicated to Thee,
>And to the Old Ways.
>Blessed be!

The child is lowered to touch the earth, then upwards again.

PRIESTESS:
>O mighty Mother of us all,
>You who have been since before the beginning,
>Witness, now, we do ask, that _____
>Has by this rite been dedicated to Thee,
>And to the Old Ways.
>Blessed be!

The Priest extinguishes the altar candles.

PRIEST
>This rite is ended,
>Merry meet and merry part!

ALL:

And merry meet again!
And may the Gods preserve the Craft!

Then follows music, dancing and feasting, with many toasts to the future of the child.

BIRTHDAY CELEBRATIONS

Everyone loves a birthday celebration. The chance to be so openly loved, honored and gifted, to be the "Star of the Show" for a day is a wonderfully enhancing experience.

The birthday marks the return of the sun to the same place (sign and degree of the zodiac) as it was at birth. So birthdays are an opportunity to remind ourselves of who we really are within our deep essential selves and to "begin again" on our lifelong assignment of being our True Selves.

An inner, meditative journey to the sun within us, as it comes into conjunction with the external sun, is helpful in aiding in the reunion of inner purpose and outer life.

On a more mundane level, birthdays can be creatively celebrated to reflect the individuality of the birthday person.

In our home birthdays are always major events. The birthday person gets to plan the menu for the entire day (this has led to some very interesting meals). He or she is greeted in the morning by many "Happy Birthday!" signs contributed by our crew of budding artists. A special hand-lettered birthday placemat, decorated with drawings of flowers and trees awaits the birthday person at the breakfast table. Vases of flowers grace the table. Exempt from regular chores, the birthday person leads a life of leisure on this day. Sometimes though, we've found it to be a good idea to involve the birthday person in the party preparations. Decorating plain white bags to be party-favor bags, filling them with the favors (seashells, feathers, stones, a special pencil, small candies, etc.), making decorations, arranging the flowers—are all good activities for a small person whose excitement level needs to be constructively channeled.

The day holds whatever birthday events have been planned. We always have a party of some kind. We've had swimming parties, hiking parties, slumber parties, skating parties, treasure-hunt parties, dress up parties and tea parties. One year our girls performed several well-rehearsed dance routines for their friends. Sometimes the children invite their friends to the party, sometimes not. We've had some pretty wonderful birthdays with just our family, plus assorted grandparents, aunts, uncles and cousins on hand.

We try to incorporate seasonal themes into the celebration. With birthdays falling on the Spring Equinox, Beltane, New Year's Eve and just past Lughnasadh, this is not difficult—the decorations are already up! The house decorations, the cake decorations and the planned activities are designed to integrate the seasonal theme with the birthday theme.

The birthday dinner is the grand event of the day. A chair at the head of the table is made into a throne by covering it with many beautiful cloths. A crown is made from stiff gold paper and glass jewels are glued onto it (our Leo children really enjoy this part). When it is time, the birthday celebrant is crowned, robed, attired in their best, and regally escorted to their place at the head of the table where they are served the dinner of their choice. A special grace is recited wherein the Gods are thanked for gifting us with this person in our lives.

We usually use the occasion of the birthday to recount birth and baby-hood stories. The little ones enjoy this very much (older ones tend to get embarrassed). We also try to use the occasion to imprint values of generosity and gratitude within both the gift givers and gift receivers.

After dinner gifts are presented, and opened, and thanks graciously given (well, most of the time!). Then the lights are turned off, candles lit on the cake, and the cake or the chosen dessert is carried in and set in front of the birthday person to the accompaniment of the birthday song. After dessert it's all over but the cleanup; and tired but happy, the birthday person retires to bed.

A birthday is a chance for us to show our love and appreciation for the birthday person. And it is an opportunity for them to practice graciousness and gratitude as well as enjoying being the center of attention for the day.

VISION QUESTS

In many native cultures part of the process of becoming an adult member of society involved seeking a vision as to one's future life's work. This involved going on a vision quest. A vision quest was serious business, a sacred quest, to be prepared for and entered into and interpreted in a serious, life-changing way. Some form of this custom would be extremely useful to a person in their late teens or early twenties, or anyone trying to achieve clarity about their life's work/path.

Material can be found in books on Native American cultures about the details of this, as well as in the books by Steven Foster and Meredith Little.

A vision quest involved the person going alone, out into nature, without food, and in some cases without water or even clothing, and crying to the Great Spirit for a vision. The idea was to disconnect the person from their normal everyday society, routine, and support system; to throw them into a totally different situation that would, by removing the background "noise," force them to be alone with themselves and with the God/Goddess/Great

Spirit-Mystery and thereby become receptive to these inner voices.

There was no set way the vision was to come. It could be a totally inner experience or come from the Great Spirit as manifested in nature, through the agency of plants, animals, weather, stars, or whatever. The person opened up to the omens, and received the messages however they were sent. After three or four days, the vision hopefully having been received, the person returned home, where the vision was recounted to whichever of the wise elders was decided to be best at helping to interpret it. But in truth sometimes the interpretation took months or even years to fully realize. Always, though, the experience of receiving the vision/message is extremely profound and empowering.

It is quite difficult to undertake such a quest in our modern, busy, city life. But it is not impossible. The easiest approach is to modify it, keeping in the essential elements of nature and isolation, and attempt to create something unique for the individual. A camping trip offers the best possibilities here; the more remote the location, the better, and the less equipment and amenities, the better, but only if one is a skilled and experienced camper with survival training or can put together a support team that is skilled and experienced.

Alternatively, arrange your quest through the agency of an organization such as the School of the Lost Borders in the Sierra Mountains of California.

The person should prepare for the quest by studying and practicing a few basic survival skills (lighting, maintaining and safely extinguishing a campfire, pitching a tent, learning about the wildlife and other things to be encountered in the chosen area, basic first aid for bites, stings, cuts, etc.) as well as fasting and learning to be alone with oneself. If hiking is to be part of the experience, physical preparation to get oneself in shape is essential. In some native cultures, the vision quest is preceded by the purification of the sweat lodge.

The practical decisions to be made concerning the vision quest are: where, when, tent or no tent, food or fasting, how many days and nights, how much water, whether or not to take reading and/or writing materials.

The person questing must have a supportive partner who will take responsibility for dropping off and picking up the quester from the chosen site, and unobtrusively bringing in water or whatever is needed.

When the quest is completed the person should take an equal number of days to reintegrate themselves into their normal routines. The experience of the quest should be savored, digested, thought about, talked about with certain close friends or advisors, or not talked about, if that is more comfortable. The experiences undergone on a vision quest are so personal, so internal, that the quester him/herself is really the only person who can understand them completely. Because of this, the experience helps one come into one's personal power and strength.

CHAPTER 18
HANDFASTING

PRENUPTIAL CELEBRATIONS

The time honored customs of bridal showers and bachelor parties are examples of rites of passage in our society for those about to change their life status through marriage. While the bridal shower concentrates on gifts for the bride personally and to take into her new household, the bachelor party is definitely designed to make the prospective groom realize he is leaving behind the single life.

Once again, as in the other times of passage, it is possible to approach this area of life in a sacred manner, without losing the sense of having a good time in the process.

Try to imagine a bridal shower preceded by the creation of sacred space, the passing around of the smudge bowl, and married women in the group talking about what the commitment and fact of being married has meant to them.

Try to imagine a bachelor party beginning in a similar way.

These occasions seem to call for little in the way of formal ritual; more of a spontaneous sharing within the framework of a stated purpose and an informally cast circle.

HANDFASTINGS

Weddings (or handfastings as we call them in the Craft) are, on the other hand, definitely a time for formal ritual. There are few who would disagree with this. Simple or elaborate, handfastings are a statement to the community that these two people have decided to form a bond and wish public recognition of the fact.

In a wedding/handfasting a contract is made between two people. Everyone else is merely witnessing the fact. For it to be legal some sort of legally recognized clergy or official is necessary, as sort of Super-Witness and to legally register the fact.

Many of the folk customs of our culture have survived in our wedding customs. The bride is "given away" by her father because in times past she was considered his possession, and the bride wears white to symbolize her purity and virginity, virtues once so dear to the patriarchy's heart. The term "honeymoon" arises from the fact that our Celtic and Anglo-Saxon ancestors used to drink plenty of mead for a month after their wedding as it was thought to induce strength and fertility (mead is made from honey). Showering the couple with rice (i.e. seeds) was thought to encourage fertility.

In this day and age, when physical fertility is not always desired, and women are not looked upon as the possessions of men to be passed from father to husband, we have the opportunity to create new customs and rituals based on equality and ecology.

The following are examples of handfasting ceremonies.

A RITE OF HANDFASTING

In this ceremony, unlike many other Wiccan ceremonies, the Quarter calling begins in the North. Sven Coman-Luger, who wrote this ritual, works in the Norse tradition of paganism. He explains that the further north one goes (in terms of latitude) the less important the sunrise position of east becomes to one's world view. In the northern lands, north is the dominant direction. Also, the North Star, by which mariners have found their way for centuries, appears in the night sky in a relatively fixed position around which the rest of the sky appears to revolve; thus underscoring the importance of North to those whose lives were as intimately involved with seafaring as were the Scandinavians.

Participants: Priest, Priestess, Bride, Groom, officers of the East, South, West and North, two friends to serve as witnesses.

The altar is in the center of the circle. At each quarter station there is a cloth on the ground to serve as a resting place for the following items: East—cord and sword; South—dagger and keys; West—bread and goblet; North—rings.

A processional song or instrumental piece is played, during which all the participants proceed to the altar area. Priestess and Priest lead the procession followed by the officers of the directions, the witnesses and finally the bridal couple. All the quarter officers carry flowers which they lay on the ground in their quarter forming a gateway. Someone (a flower girl or boy) sprinkles flowers petals around the perimeter of the circle.

PRIEST:

> As friends and family of _____ and _____ ,
> We welcome you here today.
> Come join in the celebration of this,
> The most mystical of unions between a man and a woman.

PRIESTESS:

> For that which is truly eternal is a binding of life and love.
> It is more than just flesh to flesh, it is mind to mind,
> Feeling to feeling, soul to soul, in this world and the next.
> _____ and _____ ask you to celebrate
> This joyous uniting with them now.

Pause.

PRIEST:

> Many elements make up a marriage.
> Let them be called forth.

NORTH:

> I am North, the symbol of Earth.
> Know and remember that this is the element of law,
> Of endurance, of the understanding which can not be shaken.
> I bring to your wedding the power of steadfastness.

EAST:

> I am East, the symbol of Air.
> Know and remember that this is the element of life,
> Of intelligence, of the inspiration which moves us onward.
> I bring to your wedding the power of mind.

SOUTH:

> I am South, the symbol of Fire.
> Know and remember that this is the element of light,
> Of energy, of the vigor which runs through our veins.
> I bring to your wedding the power of will.

WEST:

> I am West, the symbol of Water.
> Know and remember that this is the element of love,
> Of growth, of the fruitfulness of the earth.
> I bring to your wedding the power of desire.

PRIEST:

> These two who are joined in love, now have the desire to make
> Their bond a matter of record, so that all the world
> And the society in which they live may witness it,
> And lend to them the support of their hearts and minds.

PRIESTESS:

> For the thoughts which arise in the hearts of us all
> Are not mere fantasies, but real things;
> And each person who witnesses this marriage
> Creates a part of the structure which strengthens the bond
> Between these two who love each other.

PRIEST:

> And so in token that this, your marriage,
> Is not just a casual joining,
> I ask that some member of your community speak for you.

WITNESS #1:

> I,_____, speaking as a friend of the bride,
> Declare that the groom shall henceforth be welcomed
> Into the community of our friends.
> May our love and welcome strengthen the bond between them.

WITNESS #2:

> I,_____, speaking as a friend of the groom,
> Declare that the bride shall henceforth be welcomed
> Into the community of our friends.
> May our love and welcome strengthen the bond between them.

Music or readings here if desired. Officer of the South steps forward.

PRIEST:

> In ancient times it was a symbol of the love and trust
> A husband had for his wife that he would give to her
> Two gifts on this their wedding day:
> The keys of responsibility for his home and possessions;
> And a dagger to protect their home when he was away,
> And to stand at his side in the face of adversity.
> In recognition of this deep trust,
> _(Groom)_ gives unto _(bride)_ these two gifts.

Officer of the South gives the keys and dagger to the groom who bestows them on the bride.

Officer of the North steps forward with the rings and hands them to Priestess.

PRIESTESS:

> The exchange of rings is one of the deepest symbols of a marriage.
> It is a constant reminder, a shared touch
> Between a man and a woman.
> The circle is a symbol of the eternal.
> To give a ring to someone you love is to say
> That your love has no bounds and no end.

She gives the rings to the bride and groom.

> This bond I draw between you:
> That though you are parted in mind or in body,
> There will be a call in the core of you, one to the other,
> That nothing and no one else will answer to.
> By the secrets of earth and water is this bond woven—
> Unbreakable, irrevocable;
> By the law that created fire and wind this call is set in you,
> In life and beyond life.

The officer of the East steps forward and hands the cords to the Priest .

PRIEST:

> Each of these cords is a symbol of your lives.
> Up until this moment you have been separate
> In thought, word and action.

Ties cords.

> As these cords are tied together, your lives becomes intertwined.

Bride and groom cross hands while Priest and Priestess tie their wrists.

> As the right hand is to the left hand, may you be forever one,
> Sharing in all things, at home and abroad,
> In love and in loyalty, for all time to come.

PRIESTESS:

> _(Groom)_ , repeat after me:
> By seed and root, by bud and stem,
> By leaf and flower and fruit, by life and love,
> In the name of the Gods,
> I,_____, take thee,_____
> To my hand, my heart and my spirit.

PRIEST:

> _(Bride)_ , repeat after me;
> By seed and root, by bud and stem,
> By leaf and flower and fruit, by life and love,

In the name of the Gods,
I,_____, take thee,_____
To my hand, my heart and my spirit.

PRIEST OR PRIESTESS (or both):
By the power vested in me (us),
I now declare that you are husband and wife.

Unties hands.

Separate in fact; may you be joined in heart as in law.
I bid you exchange a kiss.

Hands cords to bride.

May you be one forever.

Officer of the West steps forward with bread and goblet, gives them to Priest and Priestess.

PRIESTESS:
Drink now of this cup to seal the vows just spoken.

Music or readings here and bread is passed around to all the guests.

PRIESTESS:
_____and_____ now bid you
Share the bounty of their household by partaking of this bread.
As each of you partake, add your blessing to this union,
And send forth a wish to the winds.

PRIEST:
May the blessings of the Old Ones, the Shining Ones
Be with you now and always.
Blessed be!

Recessional music begins and all participants leave in reverse order of entrance.

* * * * * * * * * * * * * * * * * * * *

Here is another example of a pagan wedding ceremony. Thanks to my good friends, Gryphon and Wren, for the use of this ceremony.

This wedding was held at the Summer Solstice, so the ceremony is filled with references to Solstice symbolism and mythology.

SUMMER SOLSTICE WEDDING CEREMONY

This ceremony is to be performed outside, preferably in a large, grassy area. Participants are Bride, Groom, Priestess, Priest, two people to represent each direction (East couple, etc.), and the Spiral Walk leader. To these can be added Flower Girls or Boys, Ring Bearers, etc. Bridesmaids and Grooms-men do double duty as couples representing the directions.

The altar is to be in the exact center of the ritual area. On the altar should be the usual altar equipment (two altar candles, chalice or cup, incense and holder, a bowl of salt), as well as a ribbon, a drinking glass, and a bottle of ale. The Ceremonial Broom should be nearby.

To begin, all participants and guests should line up for the Spiral Walk. The Leader is the first person in line, followed by guests, followed by wedding participants in the following order: Priest, Priestess, East couple, South couple, West couple, North couple, Flower Girl or Boy, Ring Bearer, Bride and Groom. Musicians may play during the walk, or participants can sing and chant. Flower Girl or Boy scatters flowers whenever and wherever possible.

The Leader begins the walk, leading the line counterclockwise toward the center, around the altar and back out again. All guests circle around to their places. The Direction couples stop at the direction they are to repre-sent; Priest, Priestess, Bride and Groom in their places around the altar.

Priest and Priestess bless the elements. Using the elements, they bless the bride and groom, then call for a blessing upon all those present.

Priest and Priestess step out from the circle, taking the elements and walking around the outside edge of the circle smudging and sprinkling the circle edge and the people. While this is going on, the guests join hands and breathe silently in order to ground and center. When this is complete Priest and Priestess return to the altar and set down the elements.

PRIESTESS:

> Now is the time when sweet desire weds earthy delight.
> They meet in the embrace of the seasons
> As the sun is triumphant in the sky.
> As the God and Goddess merge together in this mingling,
> So do _____ and _____ choose to merge their lives to-gether.
> As conscious recognition of their love
> They invite you to share in this ceremony with them.

PRIEST:

> Now call the Spirits of the Four Directions to honor this sacred rite!

East couple faces the East with arms extended.

EAST(1):
> Come! Mighty and Loving Spirits of the East, Powers of Air!
> Bring your blessings and protection
> To this circle and to this couple!

EAST(2):
> Come! Winged ones, dancing dawn, winds that blow!
> Bring your strength and love to this sacred ceremony
> And to this couple!

BOTH:
> Come!

They turn to face the South.

South couple faces the South with arms extended.

SOUTH(1):
> Come! Mighty and Loving Spirits of the South, Powers of Fire!
> Bring your blessings and protection to this circle
> And to this couple!

SOUTH(2):
> Come! Lion's pride, dancing heat of high noon, fire that illuminates!
> Bring your strength and love to this sacred ceremony
> And to this couple!

BOTH:
> Come!

They turn to face the West.

West couple faces the West with arms extended.

WEST(1):
> Come! Mighty and Loving Spirits of the West, Powers of Water!
> Bring your blessings and protection to this circle
> And to this couple!

WEST(2):
> Come! Swimming sea creatures, dancing dolphins, golden sunset,
> waters that wash clean!
> Bring your strength and love to this sacred ceremony
> And to this couple!

BOTH:
> Come!

They turn to face the North.

North couple faces the North with arms extended.

NORTH(1):

Come! Mighty and Loving Spirits of the North, Powers of Earth!
Bring your blessings and protection to this circle
And to this couple!

NORTH(2):

Come! Elder ones of silence, dancing mysteries of the night,
earth that gives us life!
Bring your strength and love to this sacred ceremony
And to this couple!

BOTH:

Come!

PRIEST:

Glorious nature spirits!

He extends his arms wide as if to encompass whole area.

You who lavish care upon this lovely place,
Come and join us for this sacred marriage rite
And merry Summer Solstice celebration.

PRIESTESS:

Devas!

She sweeps her arms around in a large circle.

You marvelous beings of light who animate all things!
Come and join us for this sacred marriage rite
And merry Summer Solstice celebration.

GROOM:

Gracious Lady, Goddess great!
Come and join us for this sacred marriage rite
And merry Summer Solstice celebration.

BRIDE:

Lord of the dance, God of the wildwood!
Come and join us for this sacred marriage rite
and merry Summer Solstice celebration.

PRIEST:

Each time of year comes with its own tests and rewards. This is the
time of year that Lord Sun reaches his strength and power. The opportunity for transformation is always potent at this time. It is the
power of illumination and also the moment that the Sun King starts

his journey down. The Sun is supreme. He finds his fulfillment in the caress of the Lady—Mother Earth. Together they bring their lives to fruit and flower and get ready for a new cycle. As the summer is blossoming, so do we consider the harvest in the fall. The harvest is work…and fulfillment of the promise of the spring. The couple here must be ready for the autumn of their lives as well as the summer of their days. They must be tested.

PRIESTESS:

The challenge is to love each other through all circumstances with beauty and with grace.

She ties the ribbon around their wrists and steps away.

Priest hands couple first a cup, then a bottle of wine or ale, open, but lightly corked. With tied hands they open the bottle and pour it into the cup. They face each other in salutation, pour some on the ground and drink together. Priest unties them and they set the cup and bottle on the altar.

PRIESTESS:

Summer Solstice is a time of beauty and grace,
The lushness and abundance that life offers us.
Our Sun King and Mother Earth bring fruitfulness to the land.
Let us join in our hearts as their children
Exchange promises and words of love.

Bride and groom exchange their personally written vows. Ring bearer brings rings up to the altar and gives them to Priestess.

Priestess consecrates them with salted water.

PRIESTESS:

Blessed are these rings which are a symbol
Of the eternal circle that binds this couple.

Priest consecrates the rings with incense.

PRIEST:

Blessed are these rings which are a symbol
Of the eternal love that binds us all together.

Bride and groom exchange rings with appropriate words.

PRIEST & PRIESTESS:

Then, in the name of the flowers and the fields,
The stars in the sky, the streams that flow down to the sea,
And the mystery that breathes wonder into all these things,
We now pronounce you wife and husband, man and woman!

There is a pause as bridal couple, Priest and Priestess exchange hugs and loving words.

Then the powers of the directions are invited to remain and celebrate.

EACH COUPLE AT THE QUARTERS (beginning in the East):
    Dancing dear ones of the_____,
    We would be most honored if you would stay and celebrate
    In the joy and beauty of this day!

PRIEST & PRIESTESS:
    Devas and nature spirits who dwell within this place,
    Remain with us, as you wish, to enjoy our merriment!

BRIDE & GROOM:
    God and Goddess, we would be most honored
    If you would join in our wedding festivities!

Priest explains that the broom is a symbol of blessings and good wishes. He announces that after the couple has jumped over it at the end of the ceremony, the guests will have the opportunity to wish a good wish for the couple upon the broom.

Priestess takes broom over to the East couple, who place it on the ground at the gateway to the East.

Bride and groom turn to face the guests.

BRIDE AND GROOM:
    Dear family and friends, thank you, and enjoy!

Then holding hands they run from their places and jump over the broom and out of the circle.

The East couple invites people to make a wish on the broom as they come up to congratulate the couple.

CHAPTER 19

AGE

Our society is one that worships youth at the expense of age. Much value is placed upon staying young and looking young, and cosmetic surgery, such as face-lifts, is becoming a fairly acceptable practice. While it is understandable to want to look one's best and retain youthful qualities, it is dishonest to pretend that we will never get old. But as long as our society places no value on the wisdom of the elders and routinely abuses its older citizens in so many respects (not the least of which is financially), becoming old is seen as a terrible fate.

Native societies value their elder citizens, realizing the wisdom that comes from experience. As we attempt to recreate rites of passage for ourselves, it would be valuable to learn how these events are approached in the native cultures. To address the topic of rites of passage for older women, I can do no better than to quote Brooke Medicine Eagle, a Metis Medicine Teacher whose work concerns the empowerment of women.

THE GRANDMOTHER LODGE
by Brooke Medicine Eagle

The Grandmother Lodge is the lodge of the white-haired (wisdom) women—those who have gone beyond the time of giving away the power of their blood and now hold it for energy to uphold the Law.

When our elders step across the threshold of the Grandmother Lodge, leaving their bleeding behind them, they become the Keepers of the Law. No longer is their attention consumed with the creation and rearing of their own family. In this sense they have no children, and in our ways those who are not parents to any specific child are parents to *all children.* Thus their attention turns to the children of All Our Relations; not just their own children, or the children of their friends, their clan or tribe, but the children of all the hoops: the Two-Leggeds, the Four-Leggeds, the Wingeds, the Finned, the Green Growing ones, and all others. Our relationship with this great circle of life rests ultimately in their hands. They must give-away this responsibility by modeling, teaching and sharing the living of this law in everyday life—to men, women, children—that all might come into balance.

What this means for women, in very practical terms, is that when you pass beyond menopause, you have the opportunity for a renewed and deeply powerful experience of yourself. As you drop away from the silliness and fear that has been generated by the "over the hill" cultural trance, and open yourself to the truth that lives within you—body and spirit—you will find an incredible challenge, a challenge for which you are better equipped than any other two-legged. You have the opportunity to sit in council, and using the power of the blood held among you, create a harmonious world around you.

Let me speak for a moment of a woman's moontime (menstrual) blood and its power. This blood has been shown to be among the (if not *the*) most nurturing, bioenergizing substance on Earth. When placed upon plants they are deeply nourished. In our native ways, in our ceremonies of planting and nurturing our crops, we had moon-time women (women in the days of their menses) move among the crops and give-away their blood. Always, our women gave-away this wonderful blood in an honoring way. They sat upon the ground and gave-away directly, or bled upon moss and later placed it upon the Earth to nurture and renew. Vicki Noble reminds us that this blood was the first blood offered on the altar—a most blessed gift. Then when women were no longer honored and the power of their life-giving blood was ignored, animal and human sacrifice was used to give blood on the altar.

This is the blood then that you hold among you when you no longer bleed in the moon cycle; you have passed your moontime. Elders, perhaps you have not been aware of the profound responsibility you are now to assume: if you had known you would have had the conscious opportunity to learn and deepen yourself in good relationship through your lifetime so that you might serve your people and use yourself well in these years. Younger women, you who read this now are conscious and can choose to learn and grow in this way, that you might feel ready when you, too, step into the Grandmother Lodge.

Among many of the tribes the primacy of the Law of Good Relationship was remembered and the Grandmother Lodges, or the societies within it, were known to hold the highest command. If a Peace Chief was not leading his people across the land in a way that all people and animals had good food, clear water and sheltering valleys in time of cold winds, then the

Grandmothers asked for someone new to lead; they called for someone to step forth for the people who had a better probability of doing a better job in his active work to nurture and renew the people. If a War Chief was creating such animosity among surrounding tribes that frequent attacks disrupted the life and well-being of the people, he was asked to find productive rather than destructive uses for his energy. Such was the power of the Grandmothers; they took seriously the charge to nurture and renew the people, and took action in line with it.

The Grandmother Lodge was the lodge of all postmenopausal women. Within that, smaller groups formed around their various functions. For some women, it might be the keeping of a sacred basket, for others a certain kind of healing, and for yet others the maintaining of a beauty way (art) among the people. A basket weaver might belong to a basket-makers' society and also to a society that maintained a sacred bundle (these later often came through family lineages). A woman might belong to a ceremonial Sun Dance society, and as well to a society of herbalists.

As you begin gathering with others now, you will likely have a small and mixed group, and need to determine the common interests, skills and goals among you. Perhaps you will choose a focus of speaking to children's classes about the Grandmother Lodge; or working with the Rainforest Action

Group; or creating a babysitting service for working mothers; or speaking to mens' groups on issues of harmony and good relationship—the possibilities for good are endless. Some of your time together may well be to increase your own learning and understanding—meetings to share skills with each other, to meditate and learn to listen to the Great Voices Within, gatherings to hike upon the earth or to strengthen and tone your bodies.

Something I am often asked about is those of you who have experienced amenorreah, early menopause, or hysterectomies. Where do you fit? Although I cannot say I know the exact answers, this is what makes sense to me through my own experience. The first thought I have is that you will very likely want to get a sense of the rhythm of activity/receptivity–worldly action/Great Mystery. That is your natural cycle in synchronicity with Grandmother Moon for this cycle still echoes through the waters of your body even though external bleeding does not accompany it. Deepen your experience of the moon's cycle within you; it is very powerful and useful for you and All Your Relations to reach through the veil into the Great Mystery during your bleeding and bring back vision for your people. Secondly, many of us who are younger and don't yet experience ourselves as elders are being called into the Grandmother Lodge because there is an urgent need for the awakening of this function within women. Because of the crushing of the native cultures and the loss of the women's ways, there are few who sit in these lodges and uphold the nurturing and renewing of the people. So younger, awakened ones of us are being called into the lodge through many different means. Accept it as an honor.

The final aspect of the Grandmother Lodge I would address is the rite of passage into it. Those of you surrounding a woman who is crossing this threshold will want to honor this special woman and let her know of your support of her in this time of her great responsibility. There are many ways this can be done and I will suggest only a few: ritual bathing and anointing by her closest friend, then being dressed in a white gown (for wisdom) with a red sash (to represent blood, or life force, in All Our Relations and the dedication to them) for a circle dance and feasting; an honoring of her by each woman gathered expressing her appreciation for this woman; or a special dedication from the honored one can be given. Certainly an invocation of the Goddess, of White Buffalo Woman, or the Wise Crone can be done, perhaps in the form of a guided meditation for the elder one to deepen her contact with this source of strength and wisdom. You who know her will know those aspects which have special meaning for her. Always when I do such a ritual, I include as part of the rite the charging of this woman with the primary responsibility of the nurturing and renewing of All Her Relations and remind her of the Creator's Law of Good Relationship. Among you, one already in her Grandmother Lodge might perform this function.

THE GRANDFATHER INITIATION

This passage is one of becoming an elder of the community and it may or may not be tied into becoming a grandfather in actuality. Therefore, it can occur at any time after the age of 55, depending on what the man's life responsibilities dictate. The role of grandfather will involve mentoring and advising younger men.

Present at this ritual are only the oldest men in the community. Rather than being a formal ritual, this is more of a fireside gathering, where all sit and reflect upon their lives with regard to fathering, grandfathering, being protectors, defenders, and lovers. They share food and drink, as well as their advice and insights on life as elders and grandfathers. By their words and by their stories the older men instruct the new grandfather with regard to what is required of him as an elder. This should be from their own personal experience. The person entering the Lodge of the Grandfathers brings small gifts for the others. They may bring one for him if desired.

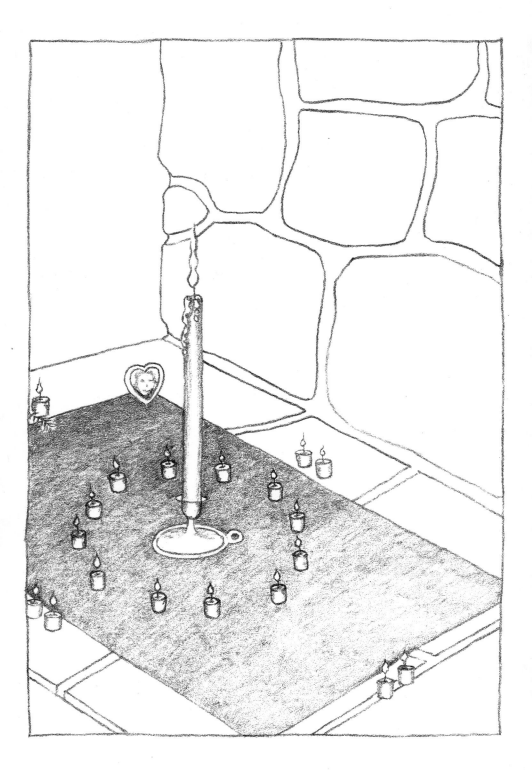

CHAPTER 20
DEATH

Preparing consciously for the passage of death is a subject matter avoided like the proverbial plague in our fearful, death-denying society. Or perhaps our society is better regarded as life-denying, since it insists on denying the reality of the living Spirit whose life permeates and animates all living beings from gnats to redwoods to stars. At any rate, the subject of preparation for death has in the most part been relegated to funereal-looking funeral directors who caution us to *be prepared* in this area of our affairs by "taking care of the arrangements" early enough so as not to leave it to the grief-stricken survivors.

What would it be like, I wonder, if we began preparing ourselves for our death early in our lives? If we were taught to regard death as a natural part of life's process, as an adventure to partake in when the right time came around for it?

Fear of the unknown is, of course, the biggest factor in our wish to deny death's existence. We can have many theories, philosophies and religious beliefs concerning death and the afterlife, but, with the possible exception of some whose powers of remembrance are great enough to allow them to remember their own previous deaths, who *really* knows what is on the other side of that particular veil?

Each person must sort this out for themselves. As for myself, I've had many dreams and remembrances that lead me to the conclusion that life after death is a reality. I have never really spent long excruciating hours in inner debate over this question; it has always been so clear and apparent to me. As to the nature of the afterlife, once again, this is open field for speculation. I have my own opinions on this subject too. And if, upon the occasion of my own death, I find that I've been terribly wrong about my opinions, I'll probably laugh and wonder at my own ignorance.

It has seemed obvious to me for some time now that such an important transition as death should be approached consciously and with reverence. Preparations should be made so that even in the case of accidental death one goes into it with some degree of consciousness.

I received some very valuable suggestions on this subject from Dolores Ashcroft Nowicki in her book *Highways of the Mind*. She has suggested that we create pathways into death, inner plane journeys created for the express purpose of bridging from this reality to the next one in a conscious way and that we build into them the suggestion that they will be automatically activated in us when we are making the death transition, even if this transition should be freakishly accidental, and that we become so familiar with them that this does indeed occur when our hour comes.

* * * * * * * * * * * * * * * * * * * *

I spent some time learning from a Mohawk woman last year, who came through my community on a teaching journey. The teaching of the Feast for the Dead was particularly meaningful for me at this time of my life. My mother was ill, and though fortunately not in a lot of pain, was bedridden, very weak, and unlikely to recover. I knew it would be a very short time until she made the transition to the spirit world. She was very much on my mind as I helped in the preparation and serving of the Feast, and at the end I, like the other participants, tossed tobacco offerings into the campfire and prayed. My prayer was that my mother's passing would be swift and easy. She passed on a few weeks later, quickly, and a few nights later sent me a dream that all was well with her.

THE MOHAWK FEAST OF THE DEAD

I will give this teaching to you as it was given to me. I do not claim to speak for the Mohawk Nation in any way, nor do I claim to be an authority on Mohawk religion and culture. As with every other ritual in this book, feel free to change it to suit your particular needs. My suggested changes follow the main body of the teaching.

This ceremonial feast is usually done within three days of a death to help the deceased person pass into the spirit realms. Friends and relatives are invited. All bring food to contribute to the feast, and a wooden gift to share. Upon arrival, these gifts are placed into a specially designated basket.

Certain special foods must be served at this feast. These foods are:

1. Three Sisters Soup (contains corn, beans and squash as the primary

ingredients, and whatever other vegetables that are brought as contributions)

2. Fruit Salad
3. Bread
4. Meat
5. Vegetables
6. Sweets, tied up in small, white-cloth bundles.

Only women are allowed to prepare and serve the feast. They begin by making tobacco offerings, honoring the four directions, and offering self and spirit and energy to this work of preparing the feast for honoring the dead person. All are smudged.

There are certain rules or traditions observed in the preparation and serving of this feast. They are:

1. No washing of any cookware, dishes, knives, etc. until the next day. Only food and hands may be washed as needed.

2. Anything that falls to the floor cannot be picked up. It is for the spirits.

3. No salt in anything. Salt keeps away the spirits and we wish to summon them.

4. Before serving those in the dining area, the food servers first prepare a plate for the deceased person (or for the spirits in general) and then plates for themselves.

5. The meal is served counterclockwise, which is the route to the inner worlds.

6. All food brought into the dining area must be served around the circle until the serving dish is empty.

7. All foods served must be eaten or taken home. Nothing should be left on the plates.

8. No cleanup until the next day.

9. The Spirit Plate is left outdoors during the night following the feast and if anything is left the next day it is fed to the birds and animals.

THE FEAST

This ceremony should take place, as stated above, as soon as possible after the death has occurred. In addition to the cook-servers, a person to act as facilitator is needed. The ceremony can be held indoors, outdoors, or in a tent or tipi, but there must be kitchen facilities close by. The dining area should be arranged so that people can sit on the floor in a circle. The feast

I attended was done in a large tipi with a fire in the center of the circle.

The cook-servers arrive about four hours before the appointed time to begin the food preparations. They bring with them the basic soup ingredients—corn, beans and squash. Before beginning the cooking, the cooks pray by making tobacco offerings (to a fire or woodstove; failing that, it can be burned as incense would be burned). They greet and honor the four directions. They offer themselves, body, spirit and energy to this work of preparing and serving the feast in honor of the dead person. After this all are smudged. Then the cook-servers adjourn to the kitchen, put the squash in the oven to bake (if it is of the hard, winter variety) and start the soup.

At the appointed time the guests arrive. They bring their food offerings to the kitchen, then go to the dining area and sit on the floor in a circle. The soup is by now bubbling away merrily on the stove, and the foods brought by the guests are added to the soup if this is appropriate. Guests can be requested to bring certain items if desired (i.e. someone can bring loaves of bread, someone else a fruit salad or vegetable dish, etc.). At the feast I participated in nothing was planned ahead and it turned out beautifully.

The cooks continue cooking and arranging the foods as the guests sit quietly in the dining area. Quiet conversation is permitted. Drumming is appropriate. About half an hour before the feast is to begin, the facilitator enters the room and joins the circle. The facilitator then begins the smudging process, followed by the teaching. The teaching communicates the reason for the feast as well as the beliefs about life, death and reincarnation. The dead person is remembered, honored, spoken about. When the teaching is finished the cook-servers enter the dining area, one at a time, and moving in a counterclockwise direction, serve the foods in the above order except for the sweets, which are not served until the very end of the whole ceremony.

No one is allowed to refuse a food, but one needn't have more than a token amount unless desired. The servers must go around the circle till the pot of food they are carrying has been emptied. The people may begin eating as soon as they receive their food. When all the courses have been served, the cook-servers come in with their own plates and join the circle after placing the Spirit Plate outdoors. The sweets are brought in at this point, but not served.

After the meal is concluded and any final teachings given or stories of the dead person shared, the gift basket is taken around by the facilitator. Everyone takes a gift from it. Then the sweets are distributed. At the end, the tobacco offering bowl is passed around and those desirous of praying and making offerings do so at this time. Or, if there is a campfire or woodstove, the prayers and offerings can be done there. When this is completed, a final bit of drumming and chanting is done to conclude the ceremony.

The next day the cook-servers come and clean up and the facilitator comes to feed any food left on the Spirit Plate to the birds and animals.

* * * * * * * * * * * * * * * * * * * *

Here is a rite that may be used for those desiring a pagan ceremony for a loved one recently passed on.

RITE FOR THE DEAD

This ceremony should be done at night, as soon as possible after the loved one has passed on.

The altar should be covered with a black cloth. Twelve white votive candles should be placed in a circle on the altar, with a red taper candle in the center of the circle. If desired, a small picture of the deceased should lean up against the red taper, or be laid upon the altar as near as possible to the red taper. Colored votives should placed at the four directions of the candle circle: yellow in the East, red in the South, blue in the West, green in the North. A sprig of evergreen, representing the everlastingness of life, should be laid between two of the candles in the West.

All present gather at the edge of the ritual area. Priest and Priestess join hands with the others and begin a spiral dance, counterclockwise, that spirals around and eventually ends with all circling the altar.

Priest and Priestess light quarter candles.

PRIEST & PRIESTESS:
> Spirit Keepers of the East (South, West, North).
> Grant safe passage to the soul of_____
> As she/he travels the path to the spirit worlds this night.
> Blessed be!

Next, twelve of those present each light one of the votives while saying:

> May your steps be sure, may your pathway be clear,
> May your way be lighted by the love of the ancestors,
> As you travel the path to the spirit worlds this night.

The bereaved now lights the red taper in the center of the circle.

BEREAVED:
> May the love and blessings
> Of the Lord and the Lady
> Be with you as you travel the path
> To the spirit worlds this night.

All present again join hands.

PRIEST:
> We gather here
> To bid farewell to a dear one
> Who must now leave us
> And travel far.
> May the blessings of the Great Mother
> And the All-Father be with you as you go!

PRIESTESS:
> Take with you the love and blessings
> Of those of us you leave behind
> As your path carries you onward.

PRIEST AND PRIESTESS (alternating):
> May your steps be sure,
> May your pathway be clear,
> May your way be lighted
> By the love of the ancestors,
> Till you reach your destination
> In the land of eternal summer.

PRIESTESS:
> There may you rest and refresh yourself;
> Till renewed, you are ready to come again
> To live upon our beautiful Mother Earth.

PRIEST:
> And may we all meet,
> And know, and remember,
> And love one another again,
> When that happy day shall come.

If so desired by the family and friends, at this time a eulogy may be given for the deceased. Any songs, poems, or readings may also be done now.

All present now place their flowers on the altar around and within the circle of the twelve candles.

PRIESTESS:
> Dear_____,
> Accept now these tokens of our love.
> Your blessed memory will live in our hearts and minds,
> Till we meet again!
> Blessed be!

All join hands and spiral dance in a clockwise direction out of the circle. The candles are left to burn out.

* *

Our beloved animal friends are truly members of our family, and, when they pass on, are deserving of a ceremony of remembrance.

RITE FOR A DEPARTED PET

This ceremony may be as formal or informal as desired. An altar should be set up with a white candle in the center. A token of the animal should be present. This can be a picture, a clipping of hair, a beloved toy, or other object. A small square of cloth and a piece of ribbon should be present.

I give thanks to you, small friend,
For the time we shared together.
I give thanks for the love we bore one another.
I give thanks for the touch of your soft fur,
Your shining eyes, kisses from your rough tongue.
I give thanks for the sound of your voice.

Go now to your rest.
I will miss you, my friend,
As you travel on your way.

But I know that someday, somewhere,
If the gods will it,
We will meet again;
And the meeting will be one of love.

May the blessings of the Lord and the Lady
Be with you as you travel on your way!

Know that my love and blessings go with you
As you travel to the Land of Eternal Summer.
Blessed be!

Now take up the token and place it within the square of cloth. Add to it a piece of your own hair or other token of yourself. Using the ribbon, tie the cloth up into a bundle, and say:

Let us be bound together in love,
That we may merry meet again!
Blessed be!

SOME FINAL WORDS

Many seasons have come and gone since I began the writing of this book; and very many seasons have passed since I began the living of it. My baby has grown into a young boy, my little girl into a preteen, my young boy into a teenager, my teenager into a young woman.

My husband and I have organized many family Sabbats, Rites of Dedication, pet funerals and birthday parties. We've had many opportunities to share with our children our pagan beliefs concerning birth and death. Along the way I've had an experience my Catholic schooling never prepared me for—raising pagan children.

My choice of the Craft as a Life Path coincided roughly with my oldest child's babyhood; so I might truthfully say that my children have all been raised to the Craft since they were born. With a Catholic grandmother and friends of other religious persuasions, the influence of other religious paths has always been part of their reality. I've tried to answer their questions about life, death and religion with honesty, and in ways that communicated to them my inner knowing and the tenets of the Craft. Only time will tell what choices they make on their own religious paths.

What I've tried hardest to instill, using the principles and rituals of the Craft as my framework, is the great wonder and mystery of life itself—as it manifests through the body of the Earth Mother—and what their relationship and responsibility to that wonder and mystery means in their everyday lives.

With my youngest child in second grade I'm far from finished with this task. Since our children are our greatest teachers, I'm sure I must have a lot left to learn since I managed to stretch them out over so wide an age range.

So perhaps in ten years time I will have written a sequel to this book, or maybe a revised edition. In the meantime, however, I hope that, in the sharing of my experiences and ideas, I have been of some help to you in the raising of your pagan children. And may you ever

BLESSED BE,
Margie McArthur
Beltane, 1993

BIBLIOGRAPHY

Ashcroft-Nowicki, Dolores. *Highways of the Mind.* London: Aquarian Press, Thorsons Publishing Group, 1987

Burland, C. A. *Echoes of Magic.* Totowa: Rowman & Littlefield, 1972

Carey, Judy and Diana Large. *Festivals, Family and Food.* Gloucestershire: Hawthorn Press, 1982

Carmichael, Alexander. *Carmina Gadelica.* Edinburgh: Lindisfarne Press, Floris Books, 1992

Connery, Clare. *In An Irish Country Kitchen.* New York: Simon & Schuster, 1992

Cosman, Madeleine Pelner. *Medieval Holidays and Festivals.* New York: Charles Scribner's Sons, Macmillan Publishing Co., 1981

Farrar, Janet and Stewart. *Eight Sabbats For Witches.* Custer: Phoenix Publishing, 1981

– – – *The Witches' Goddess.* Custer: Phoenix Publishing, 1987

Frazier, Sir James. *The Golden Bough (abridged edition).* New York: Macmillan Publishing Co., 1985

Gardner, Joy. *Color and Crystals.* Freedom: Crossing Press, 1988

Graves, Robert. *The White Goddess.* Magnolia: Peter Smith Publisher Inc., 1983

Green, Marian. *A Witch Alone.* London: Aquarian Press, imprint of Grafton Books, Harper Collins, 1991

Hole, Christina. *British Folklore and Customs.* London: Paladin, Grafton Books, Collins Publishing Group, 1978

Kindergarten Books: *Spring, Summer, Autumn, Winter, Spindrift & Gateways,* Gloucester: Wynstones Press, Brookthorpe, 1983

Medicine Eagle, Brooke. *Buffalo Woman Comes Singing.* New York: Ballantine, Random House, 1991

Noble, Vicki. *Shakti Woman.* San Francisco: Harper/San Francisco, 1991

Robertson, Lawrence. *The Year of the Goddess.* London: Aquarian Press, Thorsons Publishing Group, 1990

Ross, Anne and Don Robins. *The Life and Death of a Druid Prince.* New York: Summit Books, Simon & Schuster, 1989

Stewart, R. J. *Celtic Gods, Celtic Goddesses.* London: Blandford, imprint of Cassell, 1990

Sun Bear. *Sun Bear: The Path of Power.* New York: Prentice Hall Press, 1984.

Circle Network News, P.O. Box 219, Mt. Horeb, WI 53572
Crystal Well Magazine, San Pedro, CA (no longer being published)
Fireheart Magazine, P.O. Box 462, Maynard, MA 01754

SUGGESTED READING

CHAPTER 1 - THE SABBATS

Eight Sabbats for Witches, Janet and Stewart Farrar, Phoenix Publishing Inc., Custer, WA 98240, 1981

The Witches Way, Janet and Stewart Farrar, Phoenix Publishing Inc., Custer, WA 98240, 1984

The Witches' Goddess, Janet and Stewart Farrar, Phoenix Publishing Inc., Custer, WA 98240, 1987

The Witches' God, Janet and Stewart Farrar, Phoenix Publishing Inc., Custer, WA 98240, 1989

Magical Rites from the Crystal Well, Ed Fitch, Llewellyn Publications, St. Paul, MN 55164-0383, 1984

The Rites of Odin, Ed Fitch, Llewellyn Publications, St. Paul, MN 55164-0383, 1990

Elements of Natural Magic, Marian Green, Element Books Ltd., Dorset, England, 1989

A Witch Alone, Marian Green, The Aquarian Press, an imprint of HarperCollins Publishers, London, England, 1991

A Calendar of Festivals, Marian Green, Element Books Ltd., Dorset, England, 1992

The Wheel of the Year, Pauline Campanelli, Llewellyn Publications, St. Paul, MN 55164-0383, 1990

Ancient Ways, Reclaiming Pagan Traditions, Pauline Campanelli, Llewellyn Publications, St. Paul, MN 55164-0383, 1991

CHAPTER 3 - THE NATURAL WORLD

Animal Talk, Penelope Smith, Pegasus Publications, Pt. Reyes, CA 94956, 1982

Behaving As If The God in All Life Mattered, Machaelle Small Wright, Perelandra Ltd., Jeffersonton, VA 22724, 1983

The Perelandra Garden Workbook, Machaelle Small Wright, Perelandra Ltd., Jeffersonton, VA 22724, 1987

Color and Crystals, Joy Gardner, Crossing Press, Freedom, CA 95019, 1988

Wheels of Life, Anodea Judith, Llewellyn Publications, St. Paul, MN 55164-0383, 1988

Wheels of Light, Volume l, Rosalyn Bruyere, Bon Productions, Arcadia, CA 91006, 1989

Crystal Healing, The Next Step, Phyllis Galde, Llewellyn Publications, St. Paul, MN 55164-0383, 1988

The Art of Spiritual Healing, Keith Sherwood, Llewellyn Publications, St. Paul, MN

55164-0383, 1985

The New Healing Yourself, Joy Gardner, Crossing Press, Freedom, CA 95019, 1989

The Herbs of Life, Lesley Tierra, Crossing Press, Freedom, CA 95019, 1992

The Holistic Herbal, David Hoffman, Findhorn Press, The Park, Forres IV36 0TZ, Scotland, 1983

The Family Herbal, Barbara and Peter Theiss, Healing Arts Press, Rochester VT 05767, 1989

Natural Medicine for Children, Julian Scott, PhD., Avon Books, The Hearst Corp., New York, NY, 10016, 1990

Natural Childcare, Maribeth Riggs, Harmony Books, Crown Publishers, New York, NY 10003, 1989

The Herbal for Mother and Child, Anne McIntyre, Element Books Ltd., Dorset, England, 1992

Planetary Herbology, Michael Tierra, Lotus Press, Santa Fe, NM 87502, 1988

The Way of Herbs, Michael Tierra, Pocket Books, Simon & Schuster, New York, NY 10020, 1990

The Master Book of Herbalism, Paul Beyerl, Phoenix Publishing Inc., Custer, WA 98240, 1984

Magical Herbalism, Scott Cunningham, Llewellyn Publications, St. Paul, MN 55164-0383, 1988

Cunningham's Encyclopedia of Magical Herbs, Scott Cunningham, Llewellyn Publications, St. Paul, MN 55164-0383, 1985

Bach Flower Therapy, Mechtild Scheffer, Healing Arts Press, Rochester, VT 05767, 1988

Flower Essences and Vibrational Healing, Gurudas, Cassandra Press, San Rafael, CA 94915, 1989

CHAPTER 5 - SAMHAIN

(For the children:)

Pumpkin Moonshine, Tasha Tudor's Sampler, Tasha Tudor, David McKay Co. Inc., subsidiary of Random House, New York, NY, 10022, 1938

The Halloween Tree, Ray Bradbury, Bantam Books, Bantam/Doubleday/Dell Publishing Group, New York, NY 10103, 1972

CHAPTER 6 - YULE

A Book of Christmas, Tasha Tudor, William Collins Publishers, imprint of Institute for Humane Studies Inc., Fairfax, VA 22030-4444, 1979

Winter Story, Jill Barklem, Philomel Books, Putnam Publishing Group, New York, NY 10010, 1980

The Secret Staircase, Jill Barklem, Philomel Books, Putnam Publishing Group, New York, NY 10010, 1983

Star Mother's Youngest Child, Louise Moeri, Houghton Mifflin Co., Boston, MA 02108, 1975

CHAPTER 7 - IMBOLC

Celtic Wonder Tales, Ella Young, Floris Books, Edinburgh, Scotland, 1985

CHAPTER 8 - OSTARA

Spring Story, Jill Barklem, Philomel Books, Putnam Publishing Group, New York, NY 10010, 1980

Spring Flower Fairies, Cicely Mary Barker, Philomel Books, Putnam Publishing Group, New York, NY 10010, 1981

When the Root Children Wake Up, Helen Dean Fish, Green Tiger Press, imprint of Simon & Schuster, New York, NY 10020, 1988

CHAPTER 10 - LITHA

Summer Story, Jill Barklem, Philomel Books, Putnam Publishing Group, New York, NY 10010, 1980

Summer Flower Fairies, Cicely Mary Barker, Philomel Books, Putnam Publishing Group, New York, NY 10010, 1981

CHAPTER 11 - LUGHNASAHD

Celtic Wonder Tales, Ella Young, Floris Books, Edinburgh, Scotland, UK, 1985

The Complete Book of Straw Crafts and Corn Dollies, Doris Johnson and Alec Coker, Dover Publications, Mineola, NY 11501, 1987

CHAPTER 12 - MABON

Autumn Story, Jill Barklem, Philomel Books, Putnam Publishing Group, New York, NY 10010, 1980

Flower Fairies of the Fall, Cicely Mary Barker, Frederick Warne & Co. Inc., Penguin Group, London, England, 1990

Harry's Song, Lillian Hoban, Greenwillow Books, William Morrow & Co., New York, NY 10016, 1980

CHAPTER 13 - MOONTIDES AND MAGIC

Under The Moon, Jo Ann Ryder, Random House, New York, NY 10022, 1989

CHAPTER 15 - WOMEN'S MYSTERIES

The Wise Wound, Penelope Shuttle and Peter Redgrove, Bantam Books, Bantam/Doubleday/Dell Publishing Group, New York, NY, 10103, 1987

Dragontime, Luisa Francia, Ash Tree Publishing, Woodstock, NY 12498, 1991

Red Flower: Rethinking Menstruation, Dena Taylor, Crossing Press, Freedom, CA 95019, 1988

Flowering Woman: Moontime for Kore, Dillon and Barclay, Sunlight Productions, Sedona, AZ 86336, 1988

Daughters of Eve, Dolores Ashcroft-Nowicki, Aquarian/Thorsons, imprint of HarperCollins Publishers, London, England, 1993

Shakti Woman, Vicki Noble, Harper/San Francisco, HarperCollins Publishers, New York, NY 10022, 1991

Wise Woman Herbal for the Childbearing Year, Susun Weed, Ash Tree Publishing, Woodstock, NY 12498, 1986

Healing Wise - A Wise Woman Herbal, Susun Weed, Ash Tree Publishing, Woodstock, NY 12498, 1989

Grandmothers of the Light: A Medicine Woman's Sourcebook, Paula Gunn Allen, Beacon Press, Boston, MA 02108, 1991

The Miracle of Birth, Geoffrey Hodson, Theosophical Publishing House, Wheaton, IL 60187, 1981

Buffalo Woman Comes Singing, Brooke Medicine Eagle, Ballantine Books, Random House Inc., New York, NY 10022

Sister Moon Lodge, Kisma K. Stepanich, Llewellyn Publications, St. Paul, MN 55164-0383, 1992

The Sacred Pipe: Seven Rites of the Oglala Sioux, Joseph Epes Brown, University of Oklahoma Press, Norman, OK 73070-0787, 1953

CHAPTER 16 - MEN'S MYSTERIES

Earth Honoring, A New Male Sexuality, Robert Lawlor, Park Street Press, Rochester, VT 05767, 1989

Gods in Everyman, Jean Shinoda Bolen, Harper/San Francisco, San Francisco, CA 94111, 1989

Knights Without Armor, Aaron Kipnis, PhD, Jeremy Tarcher, Los Angeles, CA 90036, 1991

Celebrating the Male Mysteries, R. J. Stewart, Arkania Press, Bath, England, 1991

Earth God Rising, Alan Richardson, Llewellyn Publications, St. Paul, MN 55164-0383, 1988

Black Elk Speaks, John Neihardt, University of Nebraska Press, Lincoln, NE 68588-0520, 1989

The Sacred Pipe: Seven Rites of the Oglala Sioux, Joseph Epes Brown, University of Oklahoma Press, Norman, OK, 1953

Boy Into Man: A Father's Guide into the Initiation of Teenage Sons, Bernard Weiner, Transformation Press, San Francisco, CA 94110, 1992

CHAPTER 17 - YOUTH PASSAGES

The Book of the Vision Quest, Stephen Foster with Meredith Little, A Fireside Book, Simon & Schuster, New York, NY 10020, 1992

The Roaring of the Sacred River, Stephen Foster with Meredith Little, Prentice Hall Press, New York, NY 10023, 1989

The Sacred Pipe: Seven Rites of the Oglala Sioux, Joseph Epes Brown, University of Oklahoma Press, Norman, OK 73070-0787, 1953

CHAPTER 19 - AGE

Buffalo Woman Comes Singing, Brooke Medicine Eagle, Ballantine Books, Random House Inc., New York, NY 10022, 1991

Women of the 14th Moon, Dena Taylor & Amber Coverdale Sumrall, Crossing Press, Freedom, CA 95019, 1991

Menopausal Years - The Wise Woman Way, Susan Weed, Ash Tree Publishing, Woodstock, NY 12498, 1992

Sister Moon Lodge, Kisma K. Stepanich, Llewellyn Publications, St. Paul, MN 55164-0383, 1988

CHAPTER 20 - DEATH

Highways of the Mind, Dolores Ashcroft-Nowicki, Aquarian Press, Thorsons Publishing Group, Wellingborough, Northamptonshire, England, 1987

The New Book of the Dead, Dolores Ashcroft-Nowicki, Aquarian/Thorsons, an imprint of HarperCollins Publishers, London, UK, 1992

(For kids:)

The Dead Bird, Margaret Wise Brown, HarperCollins Child Books, New York, NY 10022, 1989

Saying Goodbye to Grandma, Jane Rush Thomas, Houghton Mifflin Co., Boston, MA 02108, 1990

Winter Holding Spring, Crescent Dragonwagon, Macmillan Children's Book Group, New York, NY 10022, 1990

Remember the Secret, Elizabeth Kubler Ross, Celestial Arts Publishing Co./10 Speed Press, Berkeley, CA 94707, 1988

GENERALLY GOOD READING MATERIAL FOR PAGAN CHILDREN AND THEIR ELDERS

This list is by no means exhaustive; just some of our family favorites.

(These books are appropriate for ages 10 years and up:)

THE DARK IS RISING series by Susan Cooper:

Over Sea, Under Stone, Collier Books, Macmillan Publishing, New York, NY 10022, 1986

The Dark is Rising, Collier Books, Macmillan Publishing, New York, NY 10022, 1986

Greenwitch, Collier Books, Macmillan Publishing, New York, NY 10022, 1986

The Grey King, Collier Books, Macmillan Publishing, New York, NY 10022, 1986

Silver On The Tree, Collier Books, Macmillan Publishing, New York, NY 10022, 1986

THE WRINKLE IN TIME series by Madeleine L'Engle:

A Wrinkle in Time, Dell Yearling Books, Dell Publishing, Bantam/Doubleday/Dell Publishing Group, New York, NY 10103, 1973

A Wind in the Door, Dell Yearling Books, Dell Publishing, Bantam/Doubleday/Dell Publishing Group, New York, NY 10103, 1974

A Swiftly Tilting Planet, Dell Yearling Books, Dell Publishing, Bantam/Doubleday/Dell Publishing Group, New York, NY 10103, 1981

THE CHRONICLES OF PRYDAIN series by Lloyd Alexander:

The Book of Three, Dell Yearling Books, Dell Publishing, Bantam/Doubleday/Dell Publishing Group, New York, NY 10103, 1990

The Black Cauldron, Dell Yearling Books, Dell Publishing, Bantam/Doubleday/Dell Publishing Group, New York, NY 10103, 1990

The Castle of Llyr, Dell Yearling Books, Dell Publishing, Bantam/Doubleday/Dell Publishing Group, New York, NY 10103, 1990

Taran Wanderer, Dell Yearling Books, Dell Publishing, Bantam/Doubleday/Dell Publishing Group, New York, NY 10103, 1990

The High King, Dell Yearling Books, Dell Publishing, Bantam/Doubleday/Dell Publishing Group, New York, NY 10103, 1990

THE EARTHSEA series by Ursula LeGuin:
The Wizard of Earthsea, Bantam Books, Bantam/Doubleday/Dell Publishing Group, New York, NY 10103, 1975
The Tombs of Atuan, Bantam Books, Bantam/Doubleday/Dell Publishing Group, New York, NY 10103, 1975
The Farthest Shore, Bantam Books, Bantam/Doubleday/Dell Publishing Group, New York, NY 10103, 1975
Tehanu, Bantam Books, Bantam/Doubleday/Dell Publishing Group, New York, NY 10103, 1990

THE LORD OF THE RINGS series by J.R.R Tolkien:
The Hobbit, Houghton Mifflin Co., Boston, MA 02108, 1978
The Fellowship of the Ring, Houghton Mifflin Co., Boston, MA 02108, 1982
The Two Towers, Houghton Mifflin Co., Boston, MA 02108, 1982
The Return of the King, Houghton Mifflin Co., Boston, MA 02108, 1983

THE CHRONICLES OF NARNIA by C.S. Lewis:
(Age 8 and up will appreciate these stories)
The Lion, the Witch and the Wardrobe, Collier Books, Macmillan Publishing, New York, NY 10022, 1970
Prince Caspian, Collier Books, Macmillan Publishing, New York, NY 10022, 1970
The Voyage of the Dawntreader, Collier Books, Macmillan Publishing, New York, NY 10022, 1970
The Silver Chair, Collier Books, Macmillan Publishing, New York, NY 10022, 1970
The Horse and His Boy, Collier Books, Macmillan Publishing, New York, NY 10022, 1970
The Magician's Nephew, Collier Books, Macmillan Publishing, New York, NY 10022, 1970
The Last Battle, Collier Books, Macmillan Publishing, New York, NY 10022, 1970

MYTHOLOGY AND FAIRY TALES
(For children of all ages:)
Children of Odin, Padraic Colum, Collier Books, Macmillan Publishing, New York, NY 10022, 1984
Beowulf, Kevin Crossley Holland, Oxford University Press Inc., New York, NY 10016, 1988
The Norse Myths, Kevin Crossley Holland, Pantheon Books, Random House, New York, NY 10022, 1980
The Complete Grimm's Fairy Tales, Pantheon Books, Random House, New York, NY 10022, 1972
Andersons's Fairy Tales, Hans Christian Anderson, Illustrated Junior Library, Putnam Publishing Group, New York, NY 10010, 1981
The Boys' King Arthur, Sidney Lanier, Charles Scribner's Sons, Macmillan Publishing, New York, NY 10022, 1952

Celtic Wonder Tales, Ella Young, Floris Books, Edinburgh, Scotland, 1985

Fairy and Folk Tales of Ireland, edited by W.B. Yeats, Macmillan Publishing, New York, NY 10022, 1973

The Mabinogi, trans. by Patrick Ford, University of California Press, Berkeley, 1977

Robin Hood, retold by Sara Hayes, Henry Holt & Co., New York, NY 10011, 1989

The Oz Books, L. Frank Baum and Ruth Plumly Thompson, Del Rey Books, Ballantine Books, Random House, New York, NY 10022

The "Color" Fairy Books *(Blue, Brown, Crimson, Green, Grey, Lilac, Olive, Orange, Pink, Red, Violet, Yellow)*, Andrew Lang, Dover Publishing Inc., Mineola, NY 11501

OTHER STUFF

(For very young children:)

The Witch Who Lost Her Shadow, Mary Calhoun, HarperCollins Child Books, HarperCollins, New York, NY 10022, 1979

Children of the Forest, Elsa Beskow, Floris Books, Edinburgh, Scotland, 1987

The Selkie Girl, Susan Cooper, M.K. McElderry Books, Macmillan Child Group, New York, NY 10022, 1986

The Silver Cow, Susan Cooper, Atheneum, Macmillan Publishing, New York, NY 10022, 1983

(For older children:)

The White Witch of Kynance, Mary Calhoun, HarperCollins Junior Books, New York, NY 10022, 1970

The Witch of Blackbird Pond, Elizabeth George Speare, Dell Publishing, Bantam/Doubleday/Dell Publishing Group, New York, NY 10103, 1987

A String in the Harp, Nancy Bond, Atheneum, Macmillan Publishing, New York, NY 10022, 1976

Song of the Seven Herbs, Walking Night Bear & Stan Padilla, Gold Circle Productions, P.O. Box 586, Nevada City, CA 95959, 1983

Peter Pan, J.M. Barrie, Henry Holt & Co., New York, NY 10011, 1987

Meet the Witches, Georgess McHargue, Lippincott, HarperCollins Publishers, New York, NY 10022, 1984

Wise Child, Monica Furlong, Alfred A. Knopf, Random House, New York, NY 10003, 1987

Wild Magic, Tamora Pierce, Atheneum, Macmillan Publishing, New York, NY 10022, 1992

SONG OF THE LIONESS series by Tamora Pierce

Alanna: The First Adventure, An Argo Book, Atheneum, Macmillan Publishing, New York, NY 10022, 1983

In The Hands of the Goddess, An Argo Book, Atheneum, Macmillan Publishing, New York, NY 10022, 1984

The Woman Who Rides Like a Man, Atheneum, Macmillan Publishing, New York, NY 10022, 1986

Lioness Rampant, Atheneum, Macmillan Publishing, New York, NY 10022, 1988

(Adult level - for use with children:)

Earth Child: A Guide to Earth Awareness for Parents and Teacher of Young Children, Kathryn Sheehan & Mary Waidner, Council Oak Books, Tulsa, OK 74120, 1991

Keepers of the Earth, Michael J.Caduto and Joseph Bruchac, Fulcrum Inc., Golden, CO 80401, 1988

Keepers of the Animals, Michael J.Caduto and Joseph Bruchac, Fulcrum Inc., Golden, CO 80401, 1991

Fifty Simple Things Kids Can Do To Save The Earth, Earth Works Group, Andrews and McMeel, A Universal Press Syndicate Co., Kansas City, MO 64112, 1990

RESOURCES

(Telephone numbers are provided where known.)

HERBAL CORRESPONDENCE COURSES

Rosemary Gladstar-Slick
SAGE
P.O. Box 401
East Barre, VT 05649

Lesley & Michael Tierra
EAST-WEST HERBAL CORRESPONDENCE COURSE
P.O. Box 712
Santa Cruz, CA 95061

Jeanne Rose
HERBAL STUDIES COURSE
219 Carl St.
San Francisco, CA 94117

FLOWER ESSENCES

ELLON BACH, USA, INC.
P.O. Box 320
Woodmere, NY, 11598

PEGASUS PRODUCTS, INC.
P.O. Box 228
Boulder, CO 80306

FLOWER ESSENCE SOCIETY
P.O. Box 1769
Nevada City, CA 95959
1-916-265-9163

MUSIC CASSETTE TAPES/SONGBOOKS

Phillip Wayne
4345 Sedge St.
Fremont, CA 94555

GOLDEN BOUGH
P.O. Box 818
Pacifica, CA 94044

NEMETON (tapes of Gwydion's music)
P.O. Box 1542
Ukiah, CA 95482

MAGAZINES

HAM ("How About Magic") Magazine
P.O.Box 1542
Ukiah, CA 95482

MOTHERING MAGAZINE
P.O.Box 1690
Santa Fe, NM 87504

THE DOULA
P.O. Box 71
Santa Cruz, CA 95063
1-408-646-9488

DRAGONS' QUEST
P.O. 1595
Capitola, CA 95010

GREEN EGG
P.O. Box 1542
Ukiah, CA 95482

CIRCLE NETWORK NEWS
P.O. Box 219
Mt. Horeb, WI 53572

ORGANIZATIONS

POEM (Peaceful Order of the Earth Mother; Children's subsidiary of Nemeton)
P.O. Box 1542
Ukiah, CA 95482

HANDCRAFTED, NATURAL, IMAGINATIVE TOYS

HEARTHSONG
400-B Morris St.
Sebastopol, CA 95492
1-707-829-0944

WHEATWEAVING

(supplies, instructions, products)

Morgyn Owens-Celli
FOLK TRADITIONS, LTD.
2252 Daisy Ave.
Long Beach, CA 90806

WOMEN'S MYSTERIES

Brooke Medicine Eagle
SKY LODGE
P.O.Box 121
Ovando, MT 59854
1-406-793-5730
(cassette tapes available from:
HARMONY NETWORK
P.O. Box 2550
Guerneville, CA 95446)

Susun Weed
THE WISE WOMAN CENTER
P.O. Box 64
Woodstock, NY 12498
1-914-246-8081

Kisma K. Stepanich
MOON LODGE NETWORK
204 1/2 E. Broadway
Costa Mesa, CA 92527
1-714-548-0551
(Moon Lodge Network Journal and Resource Directory - published bi-annually
at Beltane and Samhain;sample copy: $5; subscription, $15/year)

VISION QUEST INFORMATION AND ASSISTANCE

SCHOOL OF THE LOST BORDERS
P.O. Box 55
Lone Pine, CA 93545

RITES OF PASSAGE
P.O. Box 148
Sonoma, CA 95476
1-707-537-1927
Michael Bodkin, Director

WILDERNESS TRANSITIONS
70 Rodeo Ave.
Sausalito, CA 94965
1-415-331-5380
1-415-331-9558
Marilyn Riley & Betty Warren, Directors

ABOUT THE AUTHOR

Margie McArthur has been a Priestess of the Old Religion for nearly 20 years. As a mother of four children, she has also, of necessity, been a long time student of the healing arts, especially herbalism and acupressure. She served on the staff of *The Crystal Well* magazine, as Assistant Editor of *Dragon's Quest* magazine and has been a lifelong student of the Old Ways, Earth Mysteries, and Astrology. She is available for lectures, classes and Hearthkeeping workshops.

Notes

Notes

Notes

Notes

Notes